Complex PTSD Workbook

From Fear, Anxiety, Depression, and Stress
to Internal Wellbeing

Linda Hill

Table of Contents

Your Secret Gift #1

Get My Next Book

"Complex PTSD - Part 2"

(Free for a limited time)

For a limited time, and as a "Thank you" for purchasing this book, you can be added to our "Book 2 Launch List" for free so you get the second book of this series when it gets published (This book will be priced at $24.99 and I guarantee it will be a great read). Simply visit the URL below and follow the instructions. You'll be the first to get it.

Visit here:

lindahillbooks.com/ptsd

Scan QR Code:

Your Secret Gift #2

Get the Audio Version for Free

If you would like to get the audio version of this book so you can read along or listen while you are in the car, walking around, or doing other things, you're in luck. For a limited time, I've provided a link that will allow you to download this audiobook for FREE. (This offer may be removed at any time).

Step 1: Go to the URL below.

Step 2: Sign up for the 30-day free-trial membership (You may cancel at any time after, no strings attached)

Step 3: Listen to the audiobook

Visit here:

lindahillbooks.com/ptsdpromo

Scan QR Code:

How to Use this Workbook

Hello, Reader,

To use this workbook, you'll need a pen or pencil. If you are using it in an eBook format, make sure to have a notebook or pieces of paper. This book will teach you how to help yourself with C-PTSD. There will be exercises in mindfulness, meditation, self-reflection, and more. If this sounds uncomfortable to you, that is normal. But to help yourself, you're going to have to push through your discomfort and really start to dig beneath the surface of what makes your brain react the way it does. Not everything about this journey will be pretty, but when you come out on the other side (and you will), you'll have a fresh view of the world and yourself. You'll also come out from under the fog of C-PTSD and realize that you are incredible and deserve to get everything you want.

This book is not a substitute for therapy or medical

intervention. If you have suicidal thoughts, seek medical advice from a family doctor or mental health professional. Your friends, family, and loved ones are also there for you in a time of crisis, and you can seek out a spiritual leader if you are religious or contact a suicide hotline number. If you live in the United States, you can call the Natural Suicide Prevention Lifeline at 1–800–273–TALK (8255). If you are about to attempt suicide, contact 911 immediately.

This workbook will give you the tools to manage your C-PTSD. This disorder is a chronic condition, which means that it will never truly go away. However, you can develop healthy tools and habits that will help you manage your symptoms compassionately and positively.

~ ~ ~

Complex Post Traumatic Stress Disorder (C-PTSD) is a mental condition due to ongoing or consistent exposure to high-stress levels or traumatizing events. Signs and symptoms of this syndrome are intense with a wide variety of problems. The issues are similar to PTSD, but there are vital differences between the two[1].

There can be many reasons for you to have this workbook. You may be curious about C-PTSD, believe you have C-PTSD, have been diagnosed with C-PTSD, or have a loved

---

[1] Khan, N. (2022, June 24). *What Is Complex PTSD? | BetterHelp.* Better Help. https://www.betterhelp.com/advice/ptsd/what-is-complex-ptsd/

one who has been diagnosed with C-PTSD. Whatever your reason is to be reading, know that C-PTSD is a very serious disorder that can uproot the life of anyone who has it and those around them.

Post-traumatic stress disorder is a more widely known condition, and if you didn't know someone with C-PTSD before, you probably did know someone with PTSD. Although most people associate the disorder with a military condition, as many veterans have had traumatic experiences in combat, the disease also affects others who have been violently assaulted on physical or sexual levels. However, other traumas can cause PTSD as well—so don't rule anything out because the brain changes any time we experience anything where our lives are in jeopardy.

PTSD and CPSTD are emotional responses to a person's trauma, but it isn't simply a change in emotions—traumatic events cause the most disruption in the human brain. And when you are living with C-PTSD, it's like you are in constant hyper-vigilance because your body is stuck in that state of trauma.

Some of the symptoms that come along with C-PTSD are:

- Trouble regulating behavior and emotions can equate to many big, seemingly irrational emotions such as bouts of anger, rage, uncontrollable crying, or feeling numb. This problem can lead to self-injury, suicidal tendencies, sexual impulsivity, and other risk-taking behaviors.

- Amnesia and dissociation when it comes to the traumatic event. When someone dissociates, they experience a feeling of being disconnected from themselves. It could be as simple as zoning out when in a stressful situation or if you are trying to remember a traumatic experience.

- Self-perception disruptions. This turmoil can induce an inability to feel at home within yourself. A disturbance in self-perception is linked to dissociation and can manifest feelings of guilt, shame, and self-loathing.

- Confusing ideas about the person who abused you. This action involves rotating factors of idolization and loathing. It can become incredibly confusing and explosive when coupled with the previously mentioned symptoms. It is also severely harmful to the person who has C-PTSD.

- Has difficulty forming meaningful and healthy intimate relationships with others. Sadly, those with C-PTSD will re-enact the traumatic relationship with others or themselves. The traumatic experience eroded trust in people, extinguishing relationships on an intimate level.

- Have a constant and intense feeling of hopelessness and

meaninglessness. For example, if you were once deeply religious, you may disconnect from your beliefs after the trauma.

- Frequently experience physical illness and symptoms of traumatic stress. This description is labeled somatization, where the traumatic past will manifest itself in physical pain like migraines, digestive issues, and more.

If you or anyone you know experiences symptoms like these and haven't gotten a diagnosis of C-PTSD, getting checked out by a medical professional is your best bet on the road to recovery.

Using the word recovery is a tricky business. You will never be cured of C-PTSD. This disorder is chronic and lifelong. Your trauma has permanently changed your brain waves. The word "recovery" in this book talks about finding the tools to live the life you want and deserve.

As you work your way through the workbook, it is important to remember that not everything mentioned here is going to work for you. But that doesn't mean you won't find that many things do. You must pull the bits and pieces of our tips, practices, and advice that speak to you the most and fit into your lifestyle.

Close your eyes right now. Picture the person you want to be.

If you have trouble picturing that person, ask yourself a few (or all) of these questions below:

- Do you have goals and aspirations? (What are they?)

- Do you know what your purpose is?

- Are you frustrated because it seems like you always shoot yourself in the foot when you're working toward your goal?

- Do you want to be healthy?

- Do you want to feel balanced?

- Do you want to love your career?

- What is the most important thing in your life? How can you help it grow into something healthy and good?

- Do you want a healthy relationship?

- Do you prefer healthy friendships?

- Do you want a good relationship with your children (if you have them now or if you plan to have them in the future)?

- Do you want to release the constant stress and strain that lies on your shoulders every day no matter what measures you take (i.e., yoga, meditating, mindfulness practices)?

- Would you like to be kind to people?

- Learn how to be financially responsible.

- Learn how to be organized for your life.

- Learn how to build a routine for your daily schedule.

- Do you want to get comfortable with yourself so you can build confidence?

And more. Write a few questions down below if you think of any others.

- _____

- _____

- _____

- _____

- _____

- _____

- _____

- _____

- _____

- _____

Once you get a picture of how you want to live your life or who you dream of being, you've got to understand that it will take time to get to that point. There may be moments when you are at the point where you want to be, but the C-PTSD will whisper in your mind that you still aren't in the right place, time, etc.

That is the issue with C-PTSD. Every time you reach a new level, you'll find a new voice of doubt. Some days this voice will scream. On other days you'll find that you can soothe the voices with a gentle redirection and compassion for what you once went through.

Although C-PTSD studies are not as vast as those for PTSD, the research is mounting. Roughly seven percent of people in the United States have been diagnosed with PTSD[2]. In a recent survey spanning twenty-five states, sixty-one percent of these adults were found to have experienced at least one Adverse Child Experience (AEC)[3]. An adverse childhood experience is a traumatic event in one's childhood, which can

---

[2] Giourou, E., et. al. (2018). Complex posttraumatic stress disorder: The need to consolidate a distinct clinical syndrome or to reevaluate features of psychiatric disorders following interpersonal trauma? *World Journal of Psychiatry, 8*(1), 12–19. https://doi.org/10.5498/wjp.v8.i1.12

[3] Prevention, C. D. C. (n.d.). *Fast Facts: Preventing Adverse Childhood Experiences |Violence Prevention|Injury Center|CDC.* Centers for Disease Control and Prevention (CDC). Retrieved June 26, 2022, from https://www.cdc.gov/violenceprevention/aces/fastfact.html?CDC_AA_refVal=https%3A%2F%2Fwww.cdc.gov%2Fviolenceprevention%2Facestudy%2Ffastfact.html

be the start of PTSD. You've experienced AEC if you've come across any of the situations below:

- Exposure to abuse, neglect, and violence in childhood.

- Suicide in the family at a young age.

- Dependence on substances in your family.

- Family mental health disorders.

- Incarcerated family members.

- Chronic neglect or poverty.

- Unstable living environment (you've moved from place to place, etc.)

- Growing up in a crime-heavy or unsafe environment.

When you've experienced any of the above in childhood, chances are they were prolonged, complex trauma, and these situations led to AECs. While not every person who experiences an AEC will develop C-PTSD, the survey found that one in six adults experience four or more. Continued exposure to AECs can trigger the start of C-PTSD[4].

---

[4] Leonard, J. (2022, February 3). *What is complex PTSD: Symptoms, treatment, and resources to help you cope*. Medical News Daily. https://www.medicalnewstoday.com/articles/322886

Your world perspective has been skewed by the traumatic experiences you've encountered. Your worldview is unique to you, and your mind has been opened in a way that wouldn't have been if you were kept safe, warm, loved, and supported even during AECs. Once your brain has changed through triggering events, it will be difficult to see the world as you once did. If you were a child when this happened to you, you might not ever remember seeing the world differently.

This information means that you, along with medical professionals, can help yourself.

No one else can infuse healthy tools, medications (if required), and better than you can for yourself. This workbook is going to teach you how to do that. It will help you find confidence in yourself. You deserve to be released from the pain and stress caused by your trauma. You were not responsible for the traumatic experience (even if right now your brain is telling you otherwise), and you're going to realize that.

When using this workbook, understand that some things may seem weird, silly, or uncomfortable. Only through growth can you heal.

Healing isn't curing. Healing is taking care of every part of yourself instead of avoiding painful moments. You're going to discover how to nurture yourself through compassion and love. You'll develop the support you need for yourself when no one else is there to guide you.

This book is not a prescription, and to get the full effect, it may even be best to work through it with a medical professional such as a licensed therapist with experience in trauma and recovery and a family doctor to help you with medications (should you need them and feel comfortable taking them).

By the end of this book, you will have a collective understanding of C-PTSD, the symptoms, and how to manage the issues that come with the disorder. This book is not a Band-Aid for your problems. Instead, it will guide you through the difficult moments of C-PTSD. This book will provide you with a comprehensive view of C-PTSD and much more. You'll learn about symptoms of C-PTSD, The Journey of Healing, which includes: releasing the burden C-PTSD lays on your back, finding and maintaining self-esteem with yourself, and when you're in relationships. We'll also help you reframe and redirect old habits, build new ones for long-term healing, and finally make a long-term plan that can carry you through the tough times and build trust within yourself and others during the good times.

Those with C-PTSD have a hard time dealing with life. On certain days it can be a struggle just to get up, get dressed, and take care of yourself in a healthy and full of self-care. These struggles include having good relationships with people, finding success in a career, and learning to like yourself for who you are. Many people find a good rhythm for a few days, weeks, or even months, only to get knocked off the smooth path they were on because of a trigger or an anniversary of a traumatic event.

Triggers can happen around you daily. You may be living in a constant state of anxiety and hyper-vigilance to the point where you can no longer sleep, eat, or take care of yourself.

However, not all hope is lost.

When you commit to helping yourself, you show the traumatized part of you that you love and want to heal. Although that part of you is forever changed because of your chronic experiences, it doesn't have to hinder your quality of life.

The healing journey won't be an easy one. You will be taking small steps forward, and there will be setbacks. When you use this book as a guide and accept that there are darker moments in your life, you're already making progress.

Each day you wake up and decide to move forward. Even if you feel you are standing still, you will be working in the right direction.

Complex post-traumatic stress disorder does not have to rule your life. You can manage the symptoms and learn to love all parts of yourself. When you are willing to find honesty, understand that these events weren't your fault, and move into the shadows of your psyche (even if you are afraid), you give yourself the best chance at your best life.

This book was written as a guiding light. It can support you in even the darkest times. You aren't alone. You can help yourself. You have the power to create change. All you have to do is to take the first step.

You will learn how to handle the little twists and cricks with C-PTSD as long as you put the work in. You're going to find that you are stronger than you ever thought possible and realize that the growth that comes with this struggle you've dealt with for almost your entire life gives you the ability to see so many things in such a brilliant way.

Take that first step and make the first change. Lower your guard just a bit and seek all the help you need. It will be hard, but the world needs you. You offer a new light that no one else has, and we can't wait to see what you do.

Symptoms of Complex PTSD

Introduction

Complex PTSD is considered even more debilitating than its counterpart, PTSD. This complex form of PTSD requires careful treatment and special considerations. There is usually at least one other lingering disorder, which you'll see explained as comorbidity. This term is defined by a person having two or more psychological conditions simultaneously. For example, someone can have ADHD and Bipolar Disorder.

These conditions lead to all types of anxiety, addiction, eating disorders, depression, and more. When you have one disorder, the chances of you having a second or a third disorder are much higher. The psychological effects of this condition will continue to snowball and can damage certain parts of your life. While help is always available, it isn't always easy to reach out to someone, especially if you are embarrassed or have difficulty admitting that something is happening.

The problem with avoidance is that it doesn't make the condition go away, nor does it make it better. In fact, ignoring a problem, especially those of a psychological or emotional nature, only makes things so much worse. By refraining from looking too deeply at the issues, you're only lighting the fuse for an explosion. While symbolic, this explosion can lead to a host of self-harming situations such as adultery, theft, abusive behavior, tantrums, manipulation, and other items that may not be part of the person you truly are. Instead, they result from trauma that has been pushed away because of discomfort or awkward feelings.

Get Comfortable with Being Uncomfortable

One of the first steps in this workbook will be determining how to stick to your recovery plan, even when things get difficult or uncomfortable—because they will. Somedays, things will get so uncomfortable that you'll want to crawl out of your skin. But, you can take a deep breath and tell that discomfort that everything will be okay. The discomfort will not last.

And you can get comfortable with being uncomfortable.

While that sounds like an oxymoron, it is an important piece of recovery.

Without putting yourself into uncomfortable situations (not risky—there is a very distinct difference here), you're never able to grow.

If you don't grow, you will be the hamster spinning on its wheel for your life. You'll be looking forward, struggling to keep up, but never getting anywhere (and you will be unable to get off the wheel as well). You may get promoted at work, but you may still feel unsatisfied. There will be a shadow over your shoulder, a dark veil over your heart, and constant tension in your body that you'll never be able to release.

You may wake up at night and ruminate over the same thought—something that happened five, ten, or fifteen years ago—perhaps it is longer. These thoughts can keep you up and tell you lies like you aren't a good person, everything you do is wrong, or something equally as damning.

None of these things are helpful. None of them will give you the self-love and care you deserve.

So, instead, make a plan to get comfortable with discomfort.

Perhaps this will look like something different for each person. You will have to find out what works best for you. But below are a few helpful tips, suggestions, and ways to find comfort.

Take Note of Your Discomfort

This discomfort can take place in a movie theater, at a grocery store, at a football game, during a conversation, or at home.

Instead of connecting to that discomfort and pushing it away quickly, find out what caused it. Are you in a dark room? Are you talking about a specific subject? Are you seeing something that is triggering? Are there too many people around? Are there not enough people around?

Exercise One — C-PTSD Discomfort

Investigate your discomfort to find out just what is causing it.

Chances are you're going to find that you have a lot of discomfort in many places. But that is okay. If you find that you are overwhelmed by the amount of discomfort you feel, step away from it to remind yourself that you do have power in this situation. While they feel strange, your feelings don't need to dictate your thoughts and actions.

This type of self-reflection will take some work, don't beat yourself up if your feelings do take over at the beginning (or even after practicing). There are always times when we are vulnerable, and it is usually in those moments when that feeling of discomfort strikes the hardest, which can knock you back on your butt.

<u>**Helpful tools for this method:**</u>

- **Pen, pencil, journal, or laptop (whatever you are**

comfortable with). Journaling allows you to see what you are thinking. It also helps clear your mind. These two components are a crucial part of self-reflection and incredibly helpful when figuring out what makes you uncomfortable. Chances are you'll get into the habit of journaling every day for a while—this is a good practice. It will give you insight into yourself in a different way than you may not have had before. When you journal, just write your thoughts freely with no judgement—even if they feel bad. Then, when you are done writing, you can go back to see that perhaps what you are thinking and feeling aren't connected because your thoughts aren't as bad as they seem to be when they are stuck inside your head.

- **Practice mindfulness.** Mindfulness is a keyword that has been thrown around and can mean many things. However, it is going to be one of your best tools. The definition of mindfulness is being totally aware of something. However, you will focus all your attention on the present state for psychological purposes. When practicing mindfulness, you observe and experience your feelings, thoughts, and sensations without judgment[5]. This statement means that you will not push anything uncomfortable away. You will just be.

---

[5] *Definition of mindfulness*. (n.d.). Www.Dictionary.Com. Retrieved June 27, 2022, from https://www.dictionary.com/browse/mindfulness

- **Yoga**—While yoga doesn't seem to be for everyone, if you have C-PTSD, it will slow your mind down. Then you listen to your body. Think of it as another mindfulness exercise. If you've never done yoga before, don't worry. There are plenty of resources online, in books, studios, and gyms for beginners. You do not have to be extra flexible, do headstands, or become a vegan. You just have to be present in your body while focusing on a routine. If you cannot do the poses to their full potential, that is fine—it can give you something to strive for. However, when you are in yoga, it is a place to release and reflect on what you are feeling in the moment.

- **Meditation**—Grab a pillow, chair, couch, bed, or whatever you need to be comfortable for five to ten minutes a day. You can sit or lay down; this practice will not be intense meditation. You sit and listen to your thoughts with your eyes closed and your hands relaxed. That is all. It will simply be a chance for you to connect with your feelings, mind, and your body.

- **Educate yourself on C-PTSD and mindfulness.** There are plenty of places that you can research online or in print. If you've sought a therapist and believe they are the right fit for you, then ask them for some helpful resources. The more you know, the more you will understand certain reactions, emotions, feelings, etc., that you have during certain things.

You don't have to use all the tools listed above right away, nor do you have to do them for the rest of your life. Shoving a bunch of activities into your daily routine won't make you understand your disorder faster. What will likely happen is that you hyper-focus on helpful tools for a few weeks and then putter them out because you become exhausted from incorporating new practices into your life.

Instead, take it slow. It's not a battle to be fought, and it's a complex puzzle where not all the pieces have been shown to you yet. You will discover them layer by layer, and each time you unravel one and become comfortable with the process, another layer will bob to the surface and need to be addressed.

When you make the decision to manage your recovery, you're helping yourself in the best way possible. There are going to be moments of glory and moments of failure. There will be times when the C-PTSD has you in a pit of despair that it seems you will never make it out. But you will always come through. Keep trying, keep going, even when it is hard, especially when it is uncomfortable.

In this section, you will learn about the difference between PTSD and C-PTSD, gather a deeper understanding of the symptoms of C-PTSD, and see all the ways that C-PTSD impacts your daily and future life as the relationships you have with others.

What is Trauma?

Before diving into the world of PTSD and C-PTSD, you'll need to better understand what constitutes trauma. There are two types of trauma. You can have physical trauma, a product of a bodily injury that causes a wound or shock. This type of trauma is generated from an accident or violence. The other kind of trauma is psychological. When you receive trauma of the psyche, you've experienced some kind of mental injury or pain[6].

You can experience physical trauma without experiencing PTSD or C-PTSD (so long as you treat yourself kindly and indulge in self-care). But you generally cannot have psychological trauma without having physical trauma. For example, even soldiers in war have a physical trauma if unknowns constantly surround them. They have to spend a prolonged period on high alert, pushing their bodies to the limits. Not to mention the extreme danger they are in during a war. They may be either constantly shooting or being shot at.

Types of traumatic events include:

- Exposure to combat.

---

[6] Definition of trauma. (n.d.). Www.Dictionary.Com. Retrieved June 27, 2022, from https://www.dictionary.com/browse/trauma

- Childhood physical abuse.

- Sexual abuse.

- Physical assault.

- Being threatened with a weapon.

- An accident where you are physically harmed.

The list above is not exhaustive. Other events can also lead to developing PTSD. These events could be a robbery, plane crash, torture, life-threatening medical diagnosis, mugging, fire, natural disaster, terrorist attack, or other events where your life was threatened.

PTSD vs. C-PTSD

While there are many similarities between PTSD and C-PTSD, it is the key symptoms that make their diagnosis dramatically different.

Distinctions between PTSD and C-PTSD

Both PTSD and C-PTSD come from a place of deep trauma. These disorders can cause insomnia, flashbacks, and nightmares. Other symptoms create a constant fear or lack of safety even when the trauma is long past.

The central characteristic between the two is how frequently the trauma occurred.

PTSD is recognized by the DSM-V[7] in an official diagnosis, caused by a single event, and can happen at any age.

C-PTSD is caused by a long-lasting trauma that continues or repeats for months or possibly years—this trauma is often called a "complex trauma." C-PTSD is a trauma that typically happens in childhood and has not officially been recognized as a separate condition as of the latest version of the DSM-V[8].

Extra layers can be added to C-PTSD that come from the effects of racism and oppression, which increase harm to the individual. The developmental impacts of complex trauma in a person's early life are more severe than one traumatic experience. Complex trauma is created by the same or similar occurrence happening over an extended period that causes long-lasting consequences on the person's life.

Different events can cause different types of PTSD or C-PTSD. To learn more about the symptoms of PTSD and C-PTSD, continue reading below.

---

[7] *Diagnostic and Statistical Manual of Mental Disorders - The DSM-5*. (2019, April 30). The DSM5. https://www.thedsm5.com/the-dsm-5/

[8] *How a Diagnosis of Complex PTSD Differs From PTSD*. (2022, January 18). Verywell Mind. https://www.verywellmind.com/what-is-complex-ptsd-2797491

Symptoms of PTSD

Post-traumatic stress disorder is a condition triggered by a traumatic event. This event can be a singular instance that happens by experiencing it or seeing it. The common symptoms are nightmares, severe anxiety, uncontrollable or ruminating thoughts, and flashbacks.

When your thoughts ruminate, it is generally okay, and it tends to mean that you're mulling over something. However, with PTSD, thoughts that become ruminate upon tend to be that of past events you no longer have control over, minor details that "could have been" changed in a one-time event, or negative self-talk.

None of these are helpful on the road to recovery, and they can happen at any time of the day. Usually, they are unprovoked, but sometimes they come from triggers. If you wake up in the middle of the night thinking about something that has happened in the third grade, and the thought cycles over and over, you are ruminating at an unhealthy level.

Flashbacks are unique to each person. Depending on that person's brain chemistry, you can either receive flashes of the incident or feel you are transported back to the spot where you experienced the trauma. Flashbacks can include feeling the same feelings you did at the exact moment you were traumatized, or it can be a small flash of something that will take a while to understand what exactly happened.

Flashbacks are your brain's way of telling you something happened and needs to be addressed.

Many people who experience these events can have issues with adjusting back into their old lives, however, this can be a temporary problem. With self-care and by letting some time pass, things for them generally get better. However, if the symptoms worsen over time and last for months or years and interfere with your daily life—you may have PTSD.

Symptoms of PTSD can start within a range of time. They can begin one month of your experience, but may not show up until much later. Once symptoms appear, they can cause difficulties in romantic relationships, work situations, friendships, and even against yourself. Daily tasks can become increasingly hard, which can create significant problems with cleaning and taking care of yourself[9].

<u>PTSD symptoms are grouped into four types:</u>

1. Avoidance.

2. Intrusive memories.

3. Changes in emotional or physical reactions.

---

[9] *Post-traumatic stress disorder (PTSD) - Symptoms and causes.* (2018, July 6). Mayo Clinic. https://www.mayoclinic.org/diseases-conditions/post-traumatic-stress-disorder/symptoms-causes/syc-20355967

4. Negative changes in mood or thoughts.

Although you may have some symptoms, they can change and evolve. They also vary from person to person.

Avoidance

- It will lead you to avoid thoughts, emotions, and conversations about the trauma.

- It will also keep you away from places, people, and activities that remind you of what happened.

Intrusive Memories

- Memories that are unwanted and recur can generally be about a traumatic event.

- Having flashbacks—reliving the trauma as though it was happening again.

- Nightmares or upsetting dreams of trauma.

- Severe emotional distress or physical reactions when you're reminded of trauma (this instance tends to be labeled a "trigger")

Changes in emotional or physical reactions

- Stuck in a hyper-vigilant focus, always on guard for danger.

- Easily frightened or startled.

- Engage in self-destructive behavior like driving too fast or drinking too much.

- Issues with sleep.

- Difficulty concentrating.

- Show aggressive behavior, have outbursts of anger, and are constantly irritable.

Negative changes in mood and thoughts

- Feeling hopeless about the future.

- Memory loss, especially about trauma.

- Negative self-talk about yourself and thoughts about other people or the world.

- Issues maintaining friendships or close relationships.

- Detached feelings from friends and family.

- Loss of interest in things you used to enjoy.

- A tendency to feel emotionally numb.

- Have trouble expressing positive emotions[10].

Intensity of symptoms

Symptoms of PTSD can vary by day and over time. They may come up more when you are stressed out or triggered by something similar to what you went through. For example, if you come across a store that has sexual assault while reading, you may feel the panic and pain of your traumatic event.

If you find that your symptoms have lingered for longer than a month, think about contacting a mental health professional or speaking with your family doctor. The sooner you get treatment, the better it will be to prevent PTSD symptoms from worsening.

There are risk factors when it comes to PTSD. See some of the most common below:

- People of any age can have this condition.

- A stressful job can intensify PTSD symptoms, making it difficult to continue working in that chosen industry in your desired position.

- PTSD can grow into C-PTSD if you continue to put yourself in the same or similar situation that leads to

---

[10] *Post-traumatic stress disorder (PTSD) - Symptoms and causes*. (2018, July 6). Mayo Clinic. https://www.mayoclinic.org/diseases-conditions/post-traumatic-stress-disorder/symptoms-causes/syc-20355967

initial PTSD.

- You may develop issues with substance abuse by over-indulging in drugs and alcohol (mostly to numb the feelings and thoughts from your experienced trauma).

- Developing other mental disorders like anxiety, depression, or eating disorders.

- Possible suicidal thoughts or actions.

Prevention of PTSD

Symptoms may fade away depending on how you handle your traumatic event and the period after it happens. After you experience trauma, you may have symptoms that appear to be PTSD. Some of these issues could be being unable to stop thinking about what happened. You can grow angrier, depressed, anxious, guilty, and afraid about your trauma. These are all common reactions—most people who have a traumatizing event do not develop long-term PTSD.

The key is to get support to work through what happened to you. When you reach out to medical doctors and mental health professionals, they can provide you with the tools and means to alleviate the normal reaction to stress you've encountered. Speaking with your friends and family will also give you a sense of comfort. You won't have to see a mental health professional for a long time, but it is a good source to lean on until you get past your stress. If you are religious, you can always turn to your religious leaders for guidance.

The little things you do for yourself make a difference in whether or not PTSD will be long-term.

Symptoms of C-PTSD

Complex PTSD can be debilitating and overwhelming. It can affect your life in enormous ways. Those with C-PTSD have described themselves as paralyzed in fear of trauma. They always feel this way, even though they know they won't be exposed to the same event again. However, a voice always tells them "what if" or "it could happen." They spend their life living looking over their shoulder. It truly keeps them from moving on.

If this sounds like it is something similar to the things you experience, know that you are not alone. This book and many other resources like mental health professionals, online and in-print resources, guides, support groups, and hopefully, friends or family are there to help you. You just have to take that first step into wanting help.

You know that you are better than how you're performing in life now. You know that if you could just find that one "something" to get you up, moving, and motivated, you can take on the world and create something amazing for yourself and those in your life.

But there is something that continues to hold you back.

C-PTSD can keep you from achieving the life you want to live. This disorder cycles through the histrionic trauma you've already undergone, even if you've been away from it for a long time. In this way, C-PTSD is self-sabotaging. You may feel like you're on a roll—at work with a project, at home with cleaning, with friends, or in a social environment. However, it can flip in an instant. Suddenly you're so tired you can barely stay awake, even at work. Being around people makes you panic attacks, feel as though you're never going to be good enough, or try to get rid of your anxiety or depression by making your pain with alcohol, gambling, or gravitating toward many sexual partners without building any connections.

Exercise Two — What are Your C-PTSD Symptoms?

Check any symptoms that apply to you:

- Destructive or self-harming thoughts or behaviors include experimenting with drugs and alcohol or engaging in risky choices like multiple sexual partners or gambling.

- Anger issues, trouble managing your anger.

- Anxiety

- Depression

- Social isolation

- Dissociation

- Flashbacks and nightmares about your chronic trauma

- A fixation on the abuser—you may plot revenge on them or live in fear that they will find you again.

- Have suicidal thoughts, tendencies, or ideation.

  C-PTSD can be so painful that suicide seems to be the only option for a release. Know that it isn't an option. If you or someone you know has thoughts of suicide, please call the National Suicide Prevention Lifeline[11]. They are available 24 hours a day, seven days a week. The agents offer free and confidential support to anyone experiencing emotional distress, life difficulties, or who is in a suicidal crisis.

These symptoms and others like them can create a host of problems for those who have C-PTSD. They allow you to feel as though you are trapped and living in a continual state of danger or distress. Many people with C-PTSD have lost their jobs or have troubled relationships because of the lingering effects of this disorder[12].

Other things you may feel with C-PTSD can include the

---

[11] *Suicide Prevention Lifeline*. (n.d.). Suicide Prevention Lifeline. Retrieved June 27, 2022, from https://suicidepreventionlifeline.org/

[12] Khan, N. (2022, June 24). *What Is Complex PTSD? | BetterHelp*. Better Help. https://www.betterhelp.com/advice/ptsd/what-is-complex-ptsd/

following (check the box if it applies to you):

- Trust issues—you have a hard time trusting anyone. Often, your abuser was someone that you knew and trusted. This abuse shatters the ability to trust someone again without putting in some work on the matter.

- Terrible self-image (that isn't close to reality)—your perception of yourself is incredibly negative. Even though you have no valid reason to feel that way, you are amazing. However, your self-image becomes wrapped up in your trauma and will lower your self-esteem exponentially. You may even feel you deserve to be punished for something you did, thereby taking the blame onto yourself instead of directing it where it belongs.

- Hurting yourself—self-harm is a terrible way to deal with painful emotions. However, it is a way that many people attempt to escape reality. You may resort to self-harming behaviors that can also lead to your self-destruction. These behaviors can include having multiple sexual partners without building a connection or using protection or impulsivity to purchase a large item even when you don't have the money, and experimentation with drugs and alcohol. While having frequent sex with many partners is not medically harmful, you can have unplanned pregnancies and sexually transmitted diseases if you don't use protection.

Also, you don't need a connection to engage in a sexual encounter. However, this action helps you avoid intimacy, which means you're selling yourself short.

- Attachment disorders—in infancy and early childhood, you are taught how to develop deep emotional bonds and attachments. A child of neglect, abuse, or sexual assault will not have the opportunity to build these. They will have an altered sense of attachment. Although this issue makes it harder to build attachments for those with C-PTSD, it is not impossible. You'll be able to create these tools by learning healthy communication and trusting yourself to develop bonds with others (meaning that you can trust yourself to get out of a sticky situation if it is warranted.

The Treatment and Recovery of Complex PTSD

Once your brain has the trauma of sustained abuse or neglect, there isn't a possibility of a "cure." Instead, you can learn to manage symptoms and redirect your neural pathways into building a new train of thought that will allow you to live an active and healthy life. This process is a working one and will not be resolved in a short time.

Instead, you can peel away different layers of the disorder until you better understand if and how your brain works with it. You will have to decide who you want to be in the future (note that this ideal version of yourself may change throughout your recovery, which is okay. Changing your idea of who you are, showing growth and understanding of your core self telling you).

However, keeping that idea of who you see yourself as in the future will give you something to work for. You have a goal at the end of your treatment, and while you may be working on yourself for the rest of your life, you have something to look forward to.

Below you can write about how your life is now and what you want your future to be. Take time to reflect on your goals, even if you believe (right now) that they are impossible to reach. With time and treatment of your complex PTSD, you'll discover that they aren't as unreachable as you believe them.

If you have difficulty reflecting on what you may want, this activity may take a few days. Don't feel pressured to have an answer right as you read this or feel it has to be answered in one sitting. It's important to peel back those layers to find what drives you, and that will take time, especially when it has been covered up with the fog of your disorder.

Before you begin the reflection of your future self, there are a few things to understand about your recovery and the treatment of complex PTSD.

Your treatment of complex PTSD will be unique depending on the severity of your symptoms. You will not be able to tackle everything at once, and at times, you may feel overwhelmed by what you are feeling and if it seems as though there is no light at the end of the tunnel. However, know that there always is. When things seem the bleakest, it means that you're getting to the heart of the issue. It means that the light will be coming sooner than you realize it.

The treatment you undergo will depend on the experience you had, how long the experience lasted, and what exactly you went through.

Intervention with therapy, counseling, and medication may be necessary. This is only a small part of the toolbox you'll develop as you dive deeper into overcoming your C-PTSD.

First, find a counselor or therapist you feel comfortable with (not all counselors and patients are meant for each other, just like friends and romantic partners). You'll have to develop a relationship with them based on trust and have similar ideas about the world—if you are religious, you may want to find a spiritual leader in your preferred church.

You'll need to build trust with this person because there will be times when they will have to tell you some hard truths about your behavior, worldview, or reaction to certain things. Therapists are not meant to coddle. They are here to help you tackle your issues and lead you toward a healthier way of managing your symptoms.

Do not try to heal yourself alone. Build a support system around yourself, even if you have to start with someone with medical experience with your disorder. Giving yourself extra support is crucial when the weight of your trauma becomes too much. You've already been through so much. You don't have to struggle alone—finding a therapist or counselor can be an incredible way to help yourself and let your inner self know that you are worth it. You deserve to heal from your experience.

Psychotherapy is frequently called "talk therapy." The focus of this method is to stabilize your thoughts and emotions. Hence, you are free to express your feelings, improve connections with others, learn how to manage anxiety, and handle recurring memories of your trauma.

Research and stories from those who have C-PTSD have shown this type of therapy is a powerful and healthy tool to treat symptoms. You can do it online, in-person, and now even with telehealth therapy. You may have to go through a few methods before you find the right person and practice for you, but getting your thoughts out of your head and heart to release them into the world will relieve the stress and guilt that come with C-PTSD[13].

Exposure therapy focuses on the emotional and physical stress you experience when encountering distressing

---

[13] Khan, N. (2022, June 24). *What Is Complex PTSD? | BetterHelp*. Better Help. https://www.betterhelp.com/advice/ptsd/what-is-complex-ptsd/

thoughts, memories, or situations. This kind of therapy is categorized as cognitive behavior therapy (CBT), which will reduce your emotional and physical stress. Speaking with a psychologist can help you find the type of exposure therapy best for your symptoms[14].

Eye movement desensitization and reprocessing, or EMDR, is a therapy that will include a licensed therapist using this method and will also work directly with you. The therapist will have you recall a memory that troubles you. Then, they will move their finger from one side to another while you look at the movement with only your eyes. This process has proven to help desensitize you to trauma because the therapist is redirecting your focus from memory to finger motions[15]. If EMDR helps, you'll eventually be able to have the traumatic memory without experiencing emotional reactions to it[16].

Other types of psychological training can include stress inoculation (another form of CBT), focusing on redirecting how you connect stress to prolonged trauma. This process will have you learn deep breathing exercises and muscle relaxation. They are for those who need help defending themselves when they engage in negative self-talk and heightened reactions.

[14] ibid.
[15] Nanay Ph.D., B. (2022, June 22). *How and Why EMDR Works*. Psychology Today. https://www.psychologytoday.com/us/blog/psychology-tomorrow/202206/how-and-why-emdr-works
[16] Khan, N. (2022, June 24). *What Is Complex PTSD? | BetterHelp*. Better Help. https://www.betterhelp.com/advice/ptsd/what-is-complex-ptsd/

Cognitive processing therapy (CPT) focuses on trauma-related issues. This method will help you process challenging and unhealthy thoughts, beliefs, or emotions related to the experienced trauma. When you and your therapist engage in this practice, you'll create a new understanding of what happened, weakening the long-term effects that the trauma has had on your life.

Medication is always an option. While it may not be necessary at the beginning of therapy, you may discover underlying chemical imbalances that will require some sorting through. Taking medication isn't the answer for everyone. Trust the person prescribing it to you. Medication should never be used as a Band-Aid. You'll need other psychological interventions to help you manage symptoms.

Medication helps your C-PTSD brain because, since your traumatic event, it will process things (related or closely related) to the event differently. Your mind will take on a "fight or flight" response that will be quickly triggered, along with a constant state of hyper-vigilance that may cause you to shut down your emotions and spur on physical illnesses.

In some instances, medication may be necessary. However, it is up to you and your therapist to decipher. There are no specific medications that are suited directly for C-PTSD, but there have been several that are helpful with C-PTSD symptoms. Symptoms like anxiety, sleep issues, or depression. If you see a counselor or therapist and decide that medication is the right path for you (to cut through the noise C-PTSD brings), you will have to meet with a mental health professional or your family doctor to get a prescription. These professionals will be able to decipher what the best medication is for the symptoms you have.

You may also have to try several doses or types of medication before finding the right fit. Your medication usage may be temporary, or it may take longer. Just know that you're doing what is best for you now, and nothing has to stay forever. Helping yourself out means trying a host of things until you find the right pattern for you and your lifestyle[17].

Now that you have a better understanding of your treatment and recovery options, you can settle down for a few moments to think about what you want your treatment plan to look like. You can have a say in how you get help. You are the driver of your therapy and recovery. You have to do what you are comfortable with. However, remember that you are in therapy to challenge your current ideas, thoughts, behaviors, and emotions. Growth can sometimes cause discomfort, but that is different than being forced to do healing when you aren't ready to. As you go through therapy, you'll discover your boundaries and where you are okay to cross them.

Below, you can write down goals for yourself when you are healed and have a firm grasp on your healing process. Think

---

[17] Khan, N. (2022, June 24). *What Is Complex PTSD? | BetterHelp*. Better Help. https://www.betterhelp.com/advice/ptsd/what-is-complex-ptsd/

about the person you want to be. How do you see yourself? What do you hope to be doing? How do you see yourself doing it? If you have difficulty coming up with some options, see the example for suggestions or ideas on where to begin.

Examples:

- I want to feel better about myself.

- I want to go to college and graduate from college.

- I want to be a published author with a full-time professional career.

- I want to be a good parent.

- I want to be kind to people, even those who are angry.

- I want to volunteer at an animal shelter.

- I want to own a farm and keep rescue animals on it.

- I want to show my children they can do anything.

- I want to stop getting frustrated with traffic.

- I want to learn how to play the drums.

- I want to eat healthier.

- I want to teach children about art.

- I want to become a professor of sociology.

- I want to write for my local newspaper.

- I want to run a half-marathon.

- I want to grow an incredible vegetable garden.

- I want to run a clothing drive at the local school.

The list can go on. You're never going to stop making goals, especially after you find your ability to reach them. Anything you can think of is possible. You just have to find the best way to get on the right track.

Complex PTSD has a lot of symptoms. Self-sabotage is one of the worst symptoms because it stops you from being who you truly mean (and deserve). The negative voices in your head that tell you whatever happened to you is due to something you did that is wrong. The pain you feel from what happened is normal, but it is not your fault.

You can take control of your recovery. You sit behind the wheel and decide what kind of life you want. You can do it if you want to be independent and successful in running a business. If you want to find love and start a family, you'll be able to. You just have to work at the stuff in your head, create a goal, and take the first steps toward it.

Just like everything else, your happiness and goals will take work to get there, but you can totally do it.

Exercise Three — How Do You See Your Future Self?

Instructions: Take a few days and write down anything that comes to mind. When you are done, look at the goals you've set forth for yourself. Find the one that speaks to you the most, and set out a plan.

_____

_____

_____

_____

_____

_____

_____

_____

_____

_____

_____

_____

_____

_____

_____

_____

_____

_____

_____

_____

_____

_____

_____

_____

_____

_____

_____

_____

_____

_____

_____

_____

_____

_____

_____

Conclusion

Once you have the list of items, you'd like to have in the future. Make sure to take the one that speaks the loudest to you and step toward it. You can find someone to talk with about it, you can ask questions, and you can research online about your goal. Don't be afraid to say it, write about it, or talk to someone you trust.

Healing yourself from your long, traumatic experience takes time. You're going to embark on an incredible journey and get to know yourself (and others) in a brand new way. Once you accept that you have the power to manage your C-PTSD, there isn't a lot that can stop you. Even if healing creates challenges along the way, you'll work through them and keep going.

Complex PTSD didn't happen to you in one moment. It happened to you in a series of longer moments. Learning to cope with your trauma doesn't happen quickly, but you've got to reach out for help. In the next section, you'll read more about the healing journey.

Making the Decision to Recovery — The Journey of Healing

Introduction

Healing for anyone is a difficult process—it's healthy and a good thing to do, but that doesn't mean it isn't without pain and challenges. Think about a deep cut on the palm of your hand. There will be days when the scab appears, other days when the scab is itchy, sometimes it might get infected even against your best efforts, and more days when the wound is sore, red, and swollen.

While this may be an uncomfortable image to imagine, understanding that the trauma you went through has left emotional wounds that are internally larger than you even know is a good part of the healing process. These wounds will take a long time to heal, and any challenges, pain, or suffering you endure are part of your healing. Therapy and facing trauma is part of your metaphorical medicine that will remove red-hot irritation, which can fester if left untouched.

Only when you choose to suppress traumatic emotions are you truly in danger of infecting your life with the side effects.

As discussed in section one, C-PTSD comes with a host of symptoms that can affect your life in negative ways. You may even subconsciously self-sabotage because, on some deep level, your traumatic event tells you that you do not deserve happiness and cannot achieve success.

None of these ideologies are true. You deserve to be happy no matter what has happened to you or what your thoughts tell you. You deserve to reach the level you are seeking. You can be loved, successful, and at peace. You are already amazing and need to learn to love yourself.

Going through a long-term trauma scrambles our brains into a fog of uncertainty, doubt, and confusion. Because our brains become so tangled with trauma, it is hard to see things as they truly are. We really do see things through the darkened lens of what happened. When really, if we can make that step into the light, even if we only see a sliver of it initially, we can heal ourselves and learn about a different kind of inner strength that will lift us.

This section will discuss your difficulties in relationships and give a more detailed explanation of C-PTSD symptoms, along with healing exercises. It will guide you toward a decision and give you strategies to continue your journey when it becomes too difficult or painful.

You deserve the best life. You deserve to get what you want. The trauma that happens to you does not have to define you; you can take back control and learn what you're made of.

C-PTSD and Relationships

Attachment Styles

The term "secure attachment" will become something you grow familiar with. The likelihood of developing a secure attachment to anyone is terribly slim when you have C-PTSD. The problem isn't the other person and isn't technically "you" either. Instead, it results from the trauma and the idea that no one and nothing can be trusted.

Although it sounds very nihilistic, if you experience trauma, your trust has been broken on some level. You may not realize the actions you take to avoid getting close to anyone, and you may deny that you have trust issues or be fully aware of all of it.

It doesn't matter.

What matters is that secure attachment issues are on your radar.

With therapy and development, there are no direct maps. Every person's path will be different—even if they eventually go through the same thing. One person may already see their issues with attachment, while another may not find their attachment style until they tackle other symptoms that come with C-PTSD. It's not a race, and it's not a competition. There is no comparison. But if you have C-PTSD, you are more likely than not to have problems growing attached to anyone, or if you do form a bond with someone, that person may not be as good for you as it seems.

Secure attachments are the bonds you build in your early life. These connections are developed in childhood and tend to be with parents and caregivers. They are also the foundation that will shape the expectations and abilities in relationships throughout your life. The first attachments you have experienced will develop your sense of self and give you a blueprint of how relationships work. (If you see unhealthy relationships from your parents, guardians, or caregivers, you will have a harder time seeing healthy traits in others unless expressly looking for them.)

As an infant, you will uncover who you can depend on and how you depend on them. These people are charged with keeping you safe or not. Your nervous system will develop as those people are in charge of you. Their care and central nerve structure will determine if you see yourself as lovable just the way you are or will cause you to experience emotional pain you'll have to deal with later in life.

If your bond is secure, your nervous system will understand how healthy relationships are formed. You'll know that strong relationships are crucial to your well-being.

Secure attachment will guide your nervous system into self-regulation. Healthy, consistent behaviors are a part of what you deserve and how you should be treated. It will also dictate your ability to deal with problems (emotional, mental, physical, etc.) individually, because you'll never really feel alone.

If you are lucky enough to have this type of childhood or start in life, any traumatic experience you may come across may not attach itself to you in a way that can damage all your relationships—but it would crack that foundation. Again, many other factors go into how C-PTSD works in your body, mind, and emotions. C-PTSD doesn't discriminate against anyone, and each person dealing with the disorder has experienced great loss and horrible events in their life. However, if you come from a place of stability, you may understand secure attachment differently.

If you do not have a strong bedrock of love and support, you may have found, early on, that you cannot trust anyone to take care of your needs and safety. You may believe that relationships are not a place to ask for what you need and may unintentionally seek out people who prove your theory time and time again. You do not do this on purpose. This choice is ingrained deep within you, maybe even from birth. Suppose you do not know a healthy relationship while your core self is forming. In that case, it will be more difficult for you to know what one looks like or understand that you deserve to be treated with respect and have a sense of security even when you're in a vulnerable place.

Through studies and research conducted over the years, evidence has shown different degrees of emotional security with external relationships—the world of psychology calls these "attachment styles."

The attachment styles below will give you the main idea of how they form and develop over time. When you understand your attachment style, you recognize a better way to heal.

Princeton University created a study about secure attachment and attachment styles. The research discovered that only sixty percent of adults have a secure attachment style. Forty percent of subjects fell into three other styles—disorganized, avoidant, or anxious/insecure[18].

An attachment style shapes how you navigate your relationships and life throughout adulthood. Every person has a primary class, although everyone can have touches of

---

[18] *Four in 10 infants lack strong parental attachments.* (2014, March 27). Princeton University. https://www.princeton.edu/news/2014/03/27/four-10-infants-lack-strong-parental-attachments

the other types.

These four types are:

1. Anxious/insecure

2. Avoidant

3. Disorganized

4. Secure

These styles can explain how people respond when faced with communication, conflict, emotional intimacy, and relationship expectation[19].

Exercise Four — Discovering Your Attachment Style

Check the boxes that apply to you. Be honest with yourself. Knowing your attachment style will help you recover.

Group A

- I feel close to others.

- I find comfort in closeness and independence.

---

[19] Brickel, R. E., MA. (2018, October 24). *How to Heal Trauma By Understanding Your Attachment Style*. Brickel and Associates LLC. https://brickelandassociates.com/understand-attachment-style-heal-trauma/

- I communicate effectively and resolve conflicts easily.

- My relationships seem mostly stable.

- I trust your partner.

- I can share your vulnerability with my partner.

Group B

- I feel safer alone, even when I crave emotional intimacy from others.

- I grew up with an abusive primary caregiver.

- My primary caregiver waffled between love and abuse.

Group C

- I feel the urge to pull away when my partner wants emotional or physical intimacy.

- I feel closer to others when I'm away from them.

- I distance myself from stress and conflict.

- I feel emotionally distant from others.

Group D

- I become overwhelmed or anxious when I argue or disagree with a loved one.

- I pursue contact with someone, even if they've requested a break. I know they will eventually give in to me.

- I need a lot of reassurance in relationships.

- I feel unloved if I am not with my partner frequently.[20]

Once you have filled out the questionnaire above, add your score and see which group you have the most checkmarks in.

If you have checked most or all the boxes in *Group A*, you have a <u>Secure Attachment style</u>.

As discussed above, the secure attachment style means that you grew up with a solid bond between your caregivers or parents. While no one has a perfect childhood, your parents were good at being consistent. The secure attachment style allows you to develop a safe and protected feeling from the world. You were confident in their love and support and felt that your parents were emotionally open to you. You knew that if your parents left to go somewhere, they would come back.

You felt seen if you were upset, angry, happy, sad, etc. You can process distress and emotions until the disruption stops. As an adult, you can probably form closer bonds with other

---

[20] Brickel, R. E., MA. (2018, October 24). *How to Heal Trauma By Understanding Your Attachment Style*. Brickel and Associates LLC.
https://brickelandassociates.com/understand-attachment-style-heal-trauma/

adults and are comfortable with intimacy and autonomy. You develop relationships that feel good[21].

If you answered mostly in *Group B*, your attachment style is Disorganized/Unresolved Attachment.

This style is a mixture of avoidant and anxious attachment. Your caregiver could have been abusive, frightening, and behaved inappropriately toward you. You may fear them; they were not present for your safety and security. However, your child-self tells you they are your parents, and you should be loyal to them. You may want to be close to others but fear it.

Your childhood experiences have led to inconsistency and confusion in relationships on your and the other person's end.

This attachment style is the main type for those with C-PTSD

If you answered mostly in *Group C*, you have Avoidant/Dismissive Attachment.

You may have had to grow up quickly during childhood or were discouraged when expressing "unpleasant" emotions (like crying, anger, sadness, etc.). Your caregiver may have been emotionally unavailable or unaware of what you needed as a child.

---

[21] Brickel, R. E., MA. (2018, October 24). *How to Heal Trauma By Understanding Your Attachment Style*. Brickel and Associates LLC.
https://brickelandassociates.com/understand-attachment-style-heal-trauma/

In adulthood, you may now place the utmost importance on being independent and may be uncomfortable placing any dependence on others. You may pull away when allowed closeness and may not seek out relationships because sharing things with anyone else will not be safe.

If you answered mostly in *Group D*, you have Anxious/Insecure/Preoccupied Attachment.

Your caregiver throughout childhood could have responded to your needs during certain times and were not present for you at other times. Your parents could have been dealing with anxiety or issues of their own and were not available to you consistently. These actions could have left you feeling anxious and insecure since you may not have known what treatment to expect. As an adult, you may require constant reassurance and responsiveness from friends or romantic partners. Independence is not something you seek. You need dependence in a relationship to feel good about yourself. If your partner or friends are gone, your anxiety may skyrocket[22].

Attachments and Trauma

While no one is immune to trauma, the only type of attachment that does not lead to trauma is secure attachment. In the article, "How to Heal Trauma by Understanding Your Attachment Style," Robyn E. Brickel, MA, LMFT, says, "The

---

[22] ibid.

ability to regulate one's emotions isn't built in. It's taught in one's earliest relationships, ingrained throughout childhood, and practiced throughout life[23]." Brickel mentions emotional regulation "as the ability to ride the waves of life's ups and down, [and] to deal with change."

The skills needed to manage emotional regulation are more natural to those who have grown up in a house with a secure parent or caregiver. Emotional regulation is thereby more difficult for those whose childhood was more erratic.

Insecure and inconsistency with child-rearing breeds inconsistency and insecurity in your attachment style. Each of the techniques listed involved experiences when you were put in an unsafe and overwhelming environment for long periods, which led to hypo- or hyperarousal so you could protect yourself.

Experiencing stress or overwhelming despondency will traumatize you. If you don't seek to resolve this trauma, the unresolved issues of your life can lead to self-medication with drugs, alcohol, nicotine, shopping, or other ways to dull your pain and manage your emotions.

The attachment style you learned as a child isn't your fault. You grew to understand that there was a certain way to cope

---

[23] Brickel, R. E., MA. (2018, October 24). *How to Heal Trauma By Understanding Your Attachment Style*. Brickel and Associates LLC.
https://brickelandassociates.com/understand-attachment-style-heal-trauma/

with your circumstances. If you fall under the avoidance attachment style, it isn't because you did something wrong as a child. It was given to you by your primary caregiver.

Our built-in survival instincts kicked in when we saw how we were forced to live. If your environment was unsafe, you had to create a barrier of self-protection and balance to meet the insecurities provided to you. You worked with what you had. You have done the best job you could in the circumstances you were handed.

Placing blame on yourself is one of the easiest things to do, and once you're able to step away from the pain of your attachment style and C-PTSD, you may see a cycle passed down from generation to generation until it reaches you. But that is another monster to slay on a different day when you have the tools. Now you have to work on building a healthy supply of mechanisms to heal.

You can heal some of your attachment issues by finding emotionally stable relationships. Therapy is an amazing way to start healing, but a side effect of counseling is that you'll develop new ways of connecting with healthier individuals. With therapy, you can emotionally correct the problems handed to you as you build a strong tie with your therapist. That connection can build your trust in people. While a counselor's job is to be consistent and secure, they also have to be ethical, where you will discover the difference between healthy and unhealthy personal boundaries.

Healing can happen. Just because you have an attachment style born from negativity, abuse, or neglect, doesn't mean you cannot shift the type of connection you have to secure attachment. It is possible. Any style attachment can transform into a secure attachment type. It will take time and work, but you can get there—using self-reflection to become more self-aware, and the tools you learn include healthier coping skills to build strong relationships.

Exercise Five — Discovering Unhealthy Attachment Issues

Instructions: Think about a time when you were in a relationship. Without judgment, list all the unhealthy items that your partner did in the relationship—be an observer of the relationship, no need to add emotional situations. Just write what happened, how they were, and what you didn't like. Don't use simple issues like they wouldn't put the seat down or leave the butter out. Use examples that felt personal boundaries were crossed—did they steal your phone to check your text messages? Did they tell you that you couldn't accomplish something? Did you often feel your feelings, thoughts, ideas, etc., didn't matter?

After you create a list of your partner's boundary-crossing behaviors, you look at yourself—without judgment—and point out where you crossed the line, even if you were uncomfortable doing it. If you acted on instinct and later thought, "what am I doing," "this isn't right," or "I shouldn't be doing this," but you did it anyway—write it down.

See if you find a pattern developing between you and the people you are attracted to.

If you find that you avoid intimacy, reflect on those moments.

If you cannot come up with anything when you read this exercise, you can leave it blank and come back to fill it out again.

Partner's Boundaries and Lines They Crossed:

_____

_____

_____

_____

_____

_____

_____

_____

_____

_____

_____

_____

_____

_____

_____

_____

_____

_____

_____

_____

_____

_____

_____

_____

Your Boundaries and Lines You Crossed:

_____

_____

_____

_____

_____

_____

_____

_____

_____

_____

_____

_____

_____

_____

_____

_____

_____

_____

_____

_____

_____

_____

Now that you know what personal boundaries are crossed on either side, do you see a pattern in how you behave in a relationship? Do you find that your partners all have certain issues in common?

There is truth in the statement "a certain type." However, we tend to be attracted to people who are in a similar state of mind as we are. If we are unhealthy and have trouble regulating emotions, we will attract or find someone on the same level.

Abusive relationships are born from abusive relationships. To stop the cycle, we have to heal ourselves and build a new future with a better foundation.

Attachment Trauma

Now that you know what your attachment type is, it's time to break down what attachment trauma is.

Attachment trauma occurs when there is a disruption in a healthy bond between a child and their primary caregiver. A healthy attachment happens when the caregiver incorporates affection, consistency, and comfort. If the process is interrupted or if the child has unattended distress, poor attachment on the caregivers side, a lack of affection, receives abusive behavior, or an absent caregiver, attachment trauma can occur.

The consequences of attachment trauma can affect social development or spawn serious mental illnesses[24].

Attachment trauma is solely based on relational trauma, which is directly related to trauma experienced from another person or in a relationship.

And, if you struggle with relationships, there is a preconceived notion in society that states there is something specifically

---

[24] BrightQuest Treatment Centers. (2020, July 25). *What is Attachment Trauma? –*.
https://www.brightquest.com/relational-trauma/what-is-attachment-trauma/

wrong with you. Although women fall to this stigma with more severity than men do (as they are called sluts, crazy, prudes, etc.), no one is immune to the idea that the problems you have with friendships or romantic relationships, means that they are fundamentally broken in you. This statement is wrong. There is nothing wrong with you. It is how you were raised and what happened to you in your childhood.

The relationships you are born into are rooted in how you traumatically attach yourselves to others. There may be instances of highly charged emotional states, and there is an overlap between C-PTSD and attachment trauma. This type of overlap will affect you physically, mentally, and emotionally (as with evidence of the development of C-PTSD).

Physically: when faced with a similar feeling or situation, your body can instantly react. You will go into flight, fight, or freeze mode. These occurrences will be repetitive and based on your traumatic attachment. If you find yourself constantly agitated at even small things, your method of dealing with issues would be considered a "fight." If you avoid topics or events that create a similar sense of anxiety when faced with it, even in relationships, your mode of dealing will be considered "flight." If your mind goes blank and you have no sense of what to do or say when faced with these issues, your mode of physical trauma can be considered "freeze."

With CBT, your mode of handling physical occasions that emotionally remind you of your trauma can manifest over time until you can deal with inflamed situations on a healthy mental, physical, and emotional level.

However, suppose the problem is not solved with the help of internal and external therapy. In this case, your stress levels can compound and create further physical damage in invisible and visible ways. You place yourself in similar situations where you seek out more neglect and abuse.

Exercise Six — Signs of C-PTSD & Attachment Trauma:

Relationship issues are the main element and one of the most painful symptoms of C-PTSD and attachment trauma. This side effect is a direct result of your childhood trauma.

Instructions: Look at exercise five. Do you see possible unhealthy behaviors? Connect them with the symptoms below—do any of these sound like you?

- I worry about rejection constantly.

- I am afraid that no one loves me.

- I always feel alone.

- I am too attached to my friends, parents, or romantic partners.

- I worry I am in a codependent relationship.

- I often feel humiliated by the things I say, do, or how I behave.

- I tend to feel guilty about things I know I can't control.

- I have intense reactions to stressful situations.

- I don't feel like I can handle stressful situations.

- I feel constant shame.

- I worry I will do something to make my friends, family, or romantic partner abandon me.

- I cannot feel safe expressing my opinions.

- I often yell when put in a stressful situation.

- I cry frequently.

- I don't feel like I can do anything.

- I don't feel as though I am successful, even if I have a high-status position.

- I worry about making mistakes.

- I am frequently hyperfocused on others to see reactions.

- I am in a constant state of hyperarousal.

- I always look for ways that things can fall apart so I can be prepared for disappointment.

- My needs don't matter in a relationship. I will put my partner, friends, or family's needs above mine.

- I often feel depressed.

- There doesn't seem to be anything good to look forward to.

- I always have some anxiety, even if I am relaxing.

- My mind never calms down.

- I have been diagnosed with C-PTSD.

- I have been diagnosed with Borderline Personality Disorder (BPD).

- I have been diagnosed with Dissociative Identity Disorder (DID).

The symptoms above, side effects of attachment trauma, and the potential overlap of C-PTSD are only a handful of other issues that could arise. Your personal experience, coupled with your genetics, will also create an individual set of problems. While there will be generalized signs of your disorder and trauma, your road to recovery will be unique.

So, how do you heal from attachment trauma? How you manage these challenges will determine whether your relationship is healthy or unhealthy. You can develop new attachment styles with strong CBT, self-reflection, and self-awareness. You can also prevent yourself from being stuck in the same neurological patterns.

Suppose you know of your negative habits and can undo them. In that case, you'll have a greater opportunity for finding better attachments because you will be healing yourself, and your connections to healthier people will grow[25].

However, finding good friends, creating boundaries, and getting a strong romantic partner won't happen overnight. It does take work, and spending some time getting to know who you are, what you want, and where you want to be is a great place to start.

One of the biggest steps is to recognize unhealthy, self-sabotaging habits you have.

Exercise Seven — Identifying Self-Sabotaging Behaviors

Instructions: Check the behaviors that sound like you. If you've gone through the list, think about other actions that could be considered self-sabotaging[26].

---

[25] Ryder, G. (2022, January 19). *What Is Attachment Trauma?* Psych Central. https://psychcentral.com/health/attachment-trauma

[26] Gemma Stone. (2022, July). Overcoming Self-Sabotage. ToLoveThisLife.com. https://gemmastone.org/wp-content/uploads/2021/03/Overcome-Self-Sabotage-Workbook.pdf

Self-sabotage includes behaviors or thoughts that hold you back and prevent you from taking action, even on things you want to do. You can or will always find an excuse. Some of the generalized ways humans self-sabotage are:

- Being sick or getting hung over for important events.

- Procrastinating on a big project.

- Cheating on tests, diets, romantic partners, or other healthy options.

- Stuffing yourself full of junk food or purging any food you've eaten.

- Showing up late for any appointments, but especially important ones.

- Not preparing for important presentations.

- Going out, staying up all night, getting in late the day before big events.

- Ignoring important projects because you "just want to do what you want," or "it doesn't really matter to me, that much, anyway."

- Putting everything on your shoulders, not letting anyone help.

- Abusing substances like drugs, alcohol, material

possessions, and procrastination.

- Hoarding material items, not cleaning your living space, and being disorganized, you constantly lose things, documents, or bills.

- Lying, then leaning into the lie instead of being honest.

- Telling yourself that you "deserve" to have unhealthy or excessive amounts of food, alcohol, time off from work, etc.

- Over-rationalizing bad behaviors by saying something like, "They can't tell me what to do."

- Indulging in bad activities with people who don't support you in being your best self. They encourage your destruction and are considered toxic.

- You don't try to accomplish something because "it won't work out for me anyway."

- Find any reason not to do something. "It's too hard," "I won't win anyway," "I have too much on my plate," etc.

- Knowing that something is "bad," "inappropriate," or "unhealthy," but you do it anyway.

Now, write down other self-sabotaging behaviors or patterns you see in yourself.

Exercise Eight — Finding Self-Sabotaging Patterns in Your Behavior

Knowing your self-sabotaging actions forces you to acknowledge where they come from and heal your connection to that trauma.

Instructions: Look at the following patterns. Can you relate to any of these thoughts or feelings?

→ I know I am unworthy, so I self-sabotage because I don't deserve what I want.

→ This undeserving feeling leads to self-sabotage, which creates unease inside me.

→ This discomfort leads to anger, disappointment, frustration, and hopelessness, which I direct toward myself with negative self-talk.

→ The negative self-talk and destructive feelings validate my original belief about how I behave, who I am, and how I grew up as a child. Examples of these thoughts can be similar to, "I can't do anything right," "I screw up everything I touch," "There has to be something 'wrong' with me," and "I'm never going to be good enough," "I am not deserving of reaching my {insert goal here}."

→ Your undeserving feeling coupled with the beliefs of

negative self-talk will cause further self-sabotaging behaviors so you continue in the cycle of "I don't deserve to have this. I always screw everything up."

→ Which, in turn, leads you to feel anger, disappointment, frustration, and hopelessness.

→ The cycle continues to run on a hamster wheel and you'll keep running until you decide to step off of it by changing your thought process.

Do you see yourself in the patterns above? Create your self-sabotaging pattern in the empty space below. Does it look familiar or do you have other patterns that you've followed?

_____

_____

_____

_____

_____

_____

_____

_____

_____

_____

_____

_____

_____

_____

_____

_____

_____

_____

_____

_____

_____

_____

_____

_____

As with all behaviors (positive or negative), your actions will have consequences. If you continue on a negative cycle of self-sabotage, you cannot expect to heal yourself. But, by taking small steps and changing your thoughts in increments, you will slowly see the healing process.

Exercise Nine — Consequences of Your Self-Sabotaging Behavior

Instructions: Read the consequences of your actions below. Check or highlight the ones that sound like you. Once you're done, write down other developments due to self-sabotaging behaviors. Remember, these are choices you've made to stop yourself from progressing. Your actions impact your life with your career, health, relationships, finances, and more.

- You didn't get the job or promotion you wanted.

- You gave up on being healthy because junk food just tastes too good.

- You ran up your credit card bill because you just "had to" have something or needed to "shop" your stress away.

- The people in your life (co-workers, family members, managers, etc.) no longer trust you.

- You cannot count on yourself to be responsible, so no one else can trust you.

- You did something to your romantic partner, and they broke up with you.

- You continue to eat something because you've been stressed out but feel sick, bloated, or bad about yourself after you binged.

- You have no credibility at work, within your friend group, or with your family members.

- You've stopped making choices or decisions because they always turn out badly.

- You've stopped trying to reach goals because you fear making the same mistakes.

Now write out the consequences of self-sabotaging behaviors you've done. How have these actions impacted your life? Think about where you could be, who you could be with, what you could be doing if you hadn't self-sabotaged. Catch yourself when you make an excuse as to why you've not completed or even tried to accomplish a goal.

_____

_____

_____

_____

_____

_____

_____

_____

_____

_____

_____

_____

_____

_____

_____

_____

_____

_____

_____

_____

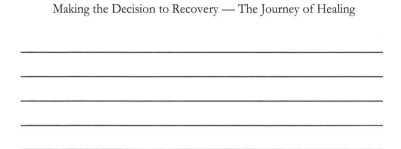

After you review your self-sabotaging patterns, consequences, and where the trauma has come from, it's time to come up with a healing solution. It's time to rewrite your script.

How do you shift your self-sabotaging patterns into healthier forms of coping skills?

First, gather the information above that you've written down. As a note, no one can recall everything they have ever done that they consider "wrong," but you're only trying to build the skills to rewire your brain when memories or intrusive thoughts pop into your mind. You don't need to compile an entire list of your lifetime of regrets, disappointments, bad habits, self-sabotaging patterns, broken promises, etc. Most people reading this book will have a lot of ammunition to choose from. If you feel like your list is long, take comfort in knowing that you are not alone.

A great step in recovery is remembering that when you pull back your ego and can admit that you have work to do on yourself, which means admitting you have made mistakes in the past and may not know everything about your actions, behaviors, words, etc. You make a commitment to work on anything that bobs to the surface of your consciousness, and you'll start to see progress in the most interesting ways.

Exercise Ten — Self-Reflection

Once you build your list of self-sabotage, attachment style, and attachment trauma, it's time to look at them through an objective lens. Ask yourself a few questions:

1. How would you react if another person told you they couldn't do something?

2. What patterns do you see playing out?

3. Where do you see your biggest fears?

4. What are the hardest things to admit to yourself?

5. What are the easiest things to admit to yourself?

6. Where does your anxiety come from?

7. Where does your anger come from?

8. What actions have you taken that have truly hurt someone?

9. What actions have you taken that only seem as though you've hurt someone but aren't really that big of a deal?

10. What signs do you see in yourself?

11. What type of attachment style do you have?

12. What opportunities have you lost?

_____

_____

_____

_____

_____

_____

_____

_____

_____

_____

_____

_____

_____

_____

_____

_____

_____

_____

_____

_____

_____

_____

Once you answer these questions on the lines above or on a separate sheet of paper, you can rework the phrasing and how you see yourself.

Exercise Eleven — Commit to Healing

Below is a list of phrases that you can say to yourself each time you have a negative thought or desire to self-sabotage[27]. Exploring the reasoning behind your actions, words, thoughts, and feelings will give you a better understanding of where the pain comes from.

When you commit to healing yourself, you're not going to put your head down and your balls to the wall and fix everything in three weeks or even three months. You have to think about how long you've lived your life with the unhealthy habits ingrained inside of you. These can't simply be wiped away, but you can start challenging them and giving yourself positive self-talk.

Each time a thought tells you, "I'm not worth it," "I'm doing something wrong," "Everyone thinks I am a joke," "I shouldn't even try," or a host of other self-deprecating thoughts, use the phrases below to test the waters and see how it feels to push back on negative, untrue statements uttered by abusive or absent caregivers.

---

[27] A. (2013, May 3). *Self-sabotage Worksheet*. EFT Masters Worldwide. https://eftmastersworldwide.com/self-sabotage-worksheet/

- I am working on being responsible.

- I do the best I can, and I am learning all the time how to be better.

- If I make a mistake, I can learn something about myself in the process.

- I want to live my life as my best self.

- I want to respect myself.

- If I don't respect myself, how can I find a way to gain respect for myself?

- I want to trust myself again.

- If I don't trust myself with something, how can I build that trust again? What actions can I take to regain my trust?

- I want to participate in things that matter to me.

- I want to find success in my life. (You can define what success looks like so you have a clear goal in mind, but don't be surprised if it changes a bit over time.)

- I want to love myself unconditionally.

- I deserve to love myself unconditionally.

- I am working on how to love myself unconditionally.

- I want to gain the respect of my friends, colleagues, and family members.

- I want to be present in every moment I can be.

- I want to be known as reliable.

- I want to do better for myself.

- I deserve to be loved.

- I deserve to get what I want.

- I deserve to be healed.

- I am worthy of love, happiness, and success.

- I can do it.

- There is always another way to get what I want, even if I fail.

- When I fail, it still means I tried to do something.

As you grow, you create phrases specifically for your negative thoughts, behaviors, and actions. That is a fantastic practice to get into. Suppose you find that you have specific thoughts not touched upon in the above examples, write down other thoughts and phrases below to challenge each negative idea that runs through your mind. The more you practice it, the easier it will come to you, and before you know it, you won't have to even think about talking yourself out of unhealthy ideas. They will come to you naturally.

_____

_____

_____

_____

_____

_____

_____

_____

_____

_____

_____

_____

_____

_____

_____

_____

_____

_____

_____

_____

_____

Healing from attachment trauma and the style that comes along with it isn't easy. You will have good days and bad ones. You will have times when you forget to challenge the ideas and emotions in your head and heart. But that's not the point. The point is that you're going to pick yourself up every time you recognize you are doing it and continue to move forward on your road to recovery.

Helpful Tips to Make Your Recovery from Attachment Trauma and Unhealthy Attachment Styles Easier:

- **Find a place or person that can give you strength.** You can list people you trust, find a support group, or look for a therapist. Any person needs connection and support, but when you're finding a way to heal from attachment trauma, you'll need a centerpiece of calmness to help you weather the storm in your head.

  Don't rely on a romantic partner for this strength. If you are already in a relationship, know that your relationship might, too, change. But, when you're going through this emotional upheaval, relying on a partner for this solidarity might have serious repercussions on both of you.

  Don't think that you need to fix everything in your relationship just because you're working on your attachment style. In fact, it's frowned upon. First, get a grip on your issues and build a stronger relationship with the people in your life.

However, don't be surprised if some people in your life now aren't with you as you grow through this practice. It's not that they don't like you or that you don't like them, but there may be shifting priorities as you get farther into healing.

Ask yourself what relationships you have that give you that feeling of security right now. What about this person or place helps you feel strong? What are the traits that allow you to feel like these are the healthy ones you'd like to follow?

- **Consider Doing Body Work.** Studies have found that people with PTSD and other attachment disorders find a lot of benefits in practicing mindfulness. Mindfulness is the state of being in the present and aware of your thoughts, feelings, and actions[28].

You cannot have a healthy mind without a healthy body, and while you cannot work on everything at once, you will be overwhelmed and set yourself up to fail. Mindfulness has been shown to help those with PTSD through breathing and grounding exercises.

These grounding exercises include yoga, meditation,

---

[28] *APA Dictionary of Psychology.* (n.d.). Https://Dictionary.Apa.Org. Retrieved July 15, 2022, from https://dictionary.apa.org/mindfulness

stretching, tapping, and others.

Mindfulness helps you disconnect your thoughts from your emotions. It guides you to understand that your thoughts cannot harm you, and if you look at them as though they are floating over your brain, like a cloud in the sky, they are easier to challenge and let go of when they are not useful[29].

When you have C-PTSD, sitting down to work on Mindfulness can be challenging. But don't give up, even when you want to. It is best to start in small bursts—sit in meditation for two minutes, then work up to five and ten. Read books on mediation to get a better understanding of it. Use streaming videos to find beginner's breathing courses. Take things slowly. It may seem like you're doing too little work, but it adds up quickly.

Don't pressure yourself. If you cannot focus, accept it and tell yourself that you will try another day. The important part of Mindfulness is that you are learning to become fully aware of how your body reacts and how your mind works.

[29] Banks, K., Newman, E., & Saleem, J. (2015). An Overview of the Research on Mindfulness-Based Interventions for Treating Symptoms of Posttraumatic Stress Disorder: A Systematic Review. *Journal of Clinical Psychology*, *71*(10), 935–963. https://doi.org/10.1002/jclp.22200

- **Use Cognitive Behavioral Therapy.** Finding a therapist who is experienced with trauma-related instances is especially important. You don't know about the ins and outs of trauma, even though you're experiencing it right now. But, a therapist and CBT treatment advise you to see things outside yourself. They can unlock memories and teach you how to move on from traumatic events. These therapists assist you through some of the most difficult times in your life, but help you understand that you'll make it through. You are strong, and you need someone to help guide your strength in the right direction[30].

You'll discover other ways to heal. Try always to be open to other people's observations, even if it makes you angry or frustrated. Chances are, if someone, even a therapist, says something that makes you cry, gets angry, or invokes any type of emotion, it means that they hit a nerve, and that nerve is attached to some part of your C-PTSD or attachment style.

Eventually, you'll be able and willing to accept change in all parts of yourself, but there will be moments of resistance. When this happens, don't get discouraged. Ride with the emotion and observe it. Ask questions like, "Why are you so

---

[30] Banks, K., Newman, E., & Saleem, J. (2015). An Overview of the Research on Mindfulness-Based Interventions for Treating Symptoms of Posttraumatic Stress Disorder: A Systematic Review. *Journal of Clinical Psychology, 71*(10), 935–963. https://doi.org/10.1002/jclp.22200

angry?" and "Where does this sadness come from?" When you mentally step away from your emotions, you can unwrap the complicated backdrop of your past. This will enable you to build an incredible future experience.

Signs You are Healing from Your Attachment Trauma

You will have many times when you question whether or not rehashing the past is worth the pain. You may have moments when you are just plain unhappy and may feel like you'll never get through the pain, but you will. Look for small signs that you are healing, and know that when your past becomes more like information and less like an inflamed emotion, you have already taken a huge step.

Acknowledging that your trauma does not define you gives you the power over your past, and you'll no longer give your issues over to anyone else.

Find other examples below to know you're on the right track.

- You trust your instincts.

- You feel safe.

- You set personal boundaries.

- Your behavior matches your beliefs and morals.

- You respond instead of reacting.

Each time you take a step toward healing, it will feel awkward and a bit uncomfortable. But, there is no one way to work on your trauma. Self-care, understanding, and kindness for yourself will take you a long way. You will find your way toward a healthier life. Trust yourself to find the right path, the right people, and the right process.

Trauma Bonding

As it goes along with attachment trauma, trauma bonding is the unhealthy connection you may feel to the person who abused you. This relationship causes a cyclical pattern of abuse. This bond was created through a mixed bag of positive reinforcement and abuse. After each abusive event, the abuser dispenses regret, expressions of love, and confusing messages that may make you feel needed or as though the instance was a consequence of something you said or did.

Nothing you say or do makes you deserve abuse.

Bonding to someone who abuses you creates a mishmash of unhealthy habits, cycles, and feelings. You may love your abuser but also feel dependent on how they treat you. The attachment you have with them is unhealthy.

Trauma bonding was first recorded by Dr. Patrick Carnes in

1997. Carnes specializes in addiction therapy and is the International Institute for Trauma and Addiction Professionals founder. Through his years, he created the trauma bonding theory, which states, "[trauma bonding is a] dysfunctional attachment that occurs in the presence of danger, shame, or exploitation." It is considered one of the nine possible reactions to traumatic events[31].

Carnes specializes in addiction therapy and is the International Institute for Trauma and Addiction Professionals founder. Through his years, he created the trauma bonding theory, which states, "[trauma bonding is a] dysfunctional attachment that occurs in the presence of danger, shame, or exploitation." It is considered one of the nine possible reactions to traumatic events.

Carnes explains that trauma bonding can happen because of how our brain changes when trauma is introduced. When your brain experiences any threat, your amygdala will be the first part that jumps to the "fight-or-flight" reaction. This response is natural and has nothing to do with being traumatized. It does, however, prepare your body to respond to the occurrence. You will either run away from the event or stay to deal with it.

Your amygdala will communicate with other areas of your brain, like your hypothalamus, which will send bursts of

---

[31] *What Is Trauma Bonding?* (2021, November 6). Verywell Mind. https://www.verywellmind.com/trauma-bonding-5207136

cortisol, the stress hormone, through your body. Your prefrontal cortex will assess if the threat is real, where the source is coming from, and determine if further action needs to happen. If your prefrontal cortex does not sense any additional danger, it will calm your body. If the risk is still present, your body will go into "survival mode" and look for other options out of the line of danger[32].

When you are exposed to trauma for a long time, your brain starts to react as though you are always in danger. The neurons and synapses become stuck in the "fight-or-flight" response method, and your mind transforms into the constant need for "getting out of the way of danger" long after you are no longer in it.

In this state, your amygdala becomes overactive, and the prefrontal cortex becomes hypoactive, which means they work against one another and cannot properly relay messages[33]. Carnes found two crucial elements to how our brains react in a traumatic situation—the response of severity and the length of time you are under "attack."

With this theory in mind, therapy can focus on how to break the bonds of trauma. These methods encourage you not to feel guilt and shame for what happened. Instead, it focuses on shifting emotions to an information-based thought process.

---

[32] *Correlation Between Structures of the Brain Function and PTSD.* (2020, February 13). Verywell Mind. https://www.verywellmind.com/what-exactly-does-ptsd-do-to-the-brain-2797210
[33] ibid.

Your trauma doesn't make you who you are; rather, it is an experience that happened to you.

Before Carnes developed his theory of trauma bonding, the idea had a different and more familiar name, Stockholm Syndrome, which did not consider all situations where an abused person bonds with their abuser and its various manifestations.

Situations of Trauma Bonding

While you can bond to your abuser in any situation—no matter how short or long the time—it is more likely to happen when your abuser waxes and wanes between love and abuse. Other scenarios play out where the abuser acts as if they didn't mean to abuse you and expects you to believe it will not happen again.

The combination of positive reinforcement and abuse mixes the signals and creates a tangled knot of messaging in your brain. You believe that your abuser isn't all "that" bad, but you also understand how dangerous they are. You may even grow to feel sorry for them or see them as the victim.

Becoming attached to your abuser is a very common trait, especially in complex types of PTSD. Should you have a bond of attachment with whoever abused you, know, there is no shame in it. The feeling and your bonded thoughts are a result of your brain seeking out methods to survive[34].

Some of the most prominent trauma bonds can happen by living or experiencing:

- Cults

- Elder abuse

- Domestic violence

- Human Trafficking

- Incest

- Kidnapping

- Sexual assault

Although it is easy to blame yourself or feel upset by the bond created between you and your abuser, over time and through therapy, you will start to see the twists and turns of cyclical abuse.

Exercise Twelve —Are you Traumatically Attached to Your Abuser?

Not all abusive events will cause you to bond with your

---

[34] *What Is Trauma Bonding?* (2021, November 6). Verywell Mind.
https://www.verywellmind.com/trauma-bonding-5207136

abuser, so you may not know if you are or not. Read the symptoms below and see if any statements apply to you.

- You make excuses or cover up an abuser's behavior.

- You lie to your family, friends, or yourself about the abuse.

- You don't feel comfortable leaving the abusive relationship.

- You don't feel as though you're able to leave the abusive relationship.

- You believe that the abuse is somehow your fault.

You are not alone in feeling this way. Trauma bonding can continue long after you remove yourself from the situation and can cause low self-esteem, depression, anxiety, fear, and self-doubt. If you stay in an abusive case, your abuse will continue and could even lead to death. If it is not dealt with, and you build a family with your abuser, the chances for intergenerational abuse increase[35].

You can break the bond.

Changing your attachment style can break the bond with your abuser. Once you remove yourself from the situation, you can

---

[35] *What Is Trauma Bonding?* (2021, November 6). Verywell Mind. https://www.verywellmind.com/trauma-bonding-5207136

prioritize moving on from the bond, so you are able to forgive yourself and let it go completely.

This statement doesn't mean that you'll forget what happened. What happened will turn into information, knowledge, and understanding about how humans work and what you can accomplish with the right tools.

The biggest step you'll need to take is removing yourself from your abusive situation. That takes courage, strength, and resolution. You deserve to be treated with kindness, compassion, and love. No matter the bond, abuse isn't a replacement for love.

If you are currently in an abusive environment, create a safety plan and then leave your situation. A safety plan involves having a safe place to go where you will have support. If you don't know where to go, there are support hotlines that can offer you help. These hotlines are open 24/7 and have people who are trained in guiding you to the right places.

Find these hotlines over the phone or online. Check out The National Domestic Violence Support Hotline[36] or Childhelp National Child Abuse Hotline[37] — these are only two examples.

---

[36] *Domestic Violence Support | The National Domestic Violence Hotline*. (2022, June 13). The Hotline. https://www.thehotline.org/
[37] *Childhelp National Child Abuse Hotline |*. (n.d.). Https://Childhelphotline.Org/. Retrieved July 15, 2022, from https://childhelphotline.org/

Conclusion

Trauma bonding, attachment styles, and attachment trauma are all part of a natural human response. None of these items is a flaw in your character. Anyone can experience these effects from abusive situations.

When you talk about your experiences, you'll be able to release any embarrassment you feel for being in the situation. You can find empathy, not pity or sympathy, from supportive people who will help you grow stronger.

You deserve to remove yourself from the abusive situation and can break any traumatic bond inflicted on you by your abuser. You do not need to stay in any case where you feel unloved, unwanted, and dominated.

By taking the first step, you decide to help yourself recover from the abuse you've experienced. It won't be an easy journey, but removing yourself from the situation and asking for help to break away from C-PTSD symptoms are the hardest parts.

The next section will discuss how to reframe the heavy burden of healing and manage the emotions that come with C-PTSD recovery.

Profound Healing — Reframing the Heavy Burden

Introduction

Hopefully, by this section, you will understand how it is possible to heal your C-PTSD. If not, comfort that recovery is possible—like any injury, some layers need to be healed. Recovery won't happen all at once, and it will likely take years to unravel all you've been through, but you can do it.

Each step you take toward facing the challenges and managing your complex PTSD symptoms is stepped in the right direction.

It's normal to hesitate when starting this process. Know that your hesitation doesn't mean that you shouldn't try to recover or that the way you are doing things is the wrong way. It just means you're unsure of the unknown.

Even when uncertainty creeps in, remind yourself that you are on a healing path for a reason. The more you help yourself, the more you can help others, and the more you can live a fulfilling life.

Ways to Heal with C-PTSD

There are a few ways to restore your brain and body when you have C-PTSD.

As a refresher:

- C-PTSD happens with long-term traumatic impacts. It impacts your body and mind and how you organize things.

- C-PTSD usually comes from relational trauma, which is trauma that happens in a close relationship.

- When recovering from C-PTSD, you must reach out to a professional for help. Find a therapist well-versed in C-PTSD and trauma.

The human brain is an interesting organ. When it works correctly, humans can achieve incredible feats. However, when a mind is thrown out of sync because of trauma or another cataclysmic event, your brain reorders itself to "protect" you from the trauma. But, when someone experiences prolonged trauma, the mind will get stuck in that state of protection.

This state means that your brain will cease to function as it was designed, and instead, you'll have a host of operations that don't work with your body or personality. Things can change drastically, and you may have some intense behaviors that seem "normal" but are blown out of proportion to the reality of the event or create other issues for you.

For example, a child who lives in a home where they never know when they will be able to eat will learn to store food. But, their brain gets stuck in that mindset long after they've been taken out of that situation—even if the food is plentiful in their new environment. The lack of food for a drawn-out period can essentially create a food disorder by having the child binge on food. Not because they don't understand that the food won't be there any longer, but because their brains are wired to tell them it's the only way to stay "safe," even when their environment is safe.

This behavior can cause a variety of issues with not only food disorders, but the child can steal food when anxious, which can lead to stealing other things. Also, extra food and stealing it can lead to stomach, teeth, and social issues.

When the child was younger, they needed to hoard food, but now that they were removed from the situation, their hoarding continues.

It's not the child's fault they were put in that circumstance, but they are left with the aftermath.

Trying to redirect these behaviors is a movement toward taking back control of your brain and body.

While this workbook is only a guidepost to help you work through your possible C-PTSD symptoms, it is important and helpful to understand where some of your brain's "protection" modes have kicked in. Below is an exercise to help you suss out parts of this multifaceted issue. If you worry that going through this exercise will trigger a heightened emotional reaction for you, make sure to do this exercise with a professional in the room. Having a professional's support will help you deconstruct some of your heavier feelings, should you spiral out of control.

Exercise Thirteen—Where Does Your Brain Have You Stuck?

Instructions: Think about your trauma—it may be difficult, but remember to breathe through the pain—answer the following questions in the space below.

1. What were you deprived of most when you were stuck in your prolonged event?

2. Where were you lacking the most control?

3. What memories stick out to you the most? How did you

feel about yourself?

4. Where do you lack the most control now (For example, overeating, undereating, hypersexuality, stealing, emotional numbness, etc.)?

5. Do you see a connection between your lack of control in your present and the trauma you faced?

6. Where do you feel that you lose the most control?

7. Do you become hyperaware in any specific situation?

8. Do you become disassociated from any specific circumstance? (To dissociate is when your mind and body split off. You will tend to feel like your mind is separated from your body.)

9. Do you find yourself doing self-destructive things? (This doesn't have to be big, but small things can add up over time, like buying something that is "only $5.00." Which winds up pushing your credit card limit over the max.)

10. What areas in your life are the hardest to focus on? What circumstances do you come across that make it hard for you to concentrate?

Take each of these answers one by one. There is no need to rush through them, nor is there a reason to answer them all simultaneously. If you feel overwhelmed by any of these questions, step away and only revisit them with your mental health provider or when you've talked through the feelings with your mental health specialist. You don't need to tackle this alone—understanding your actions through self-reflection is a huge part of your recovery and hitting on all those points at once is unhealthy.

Once you're ready to answer them, you can fill them out on paper or use the space below.

_____

_____

_____

_____

_____

_____

_____

_____

_____

_____

_____

_____

_____

_____

_____

_____

_____

_____

_____

_____

_____

_____

_____

_____

_____

_____

_____

_____

_____

_____

_____

_____

_____

_____

_____

_____

Once you get an idea of where your trauma "pain points" are, you can start to work on a treatment plan with your therapist.

What is the Treatment for C-PTSD?

Because the layers of C-PTSD trauma are hidden, they can show themselves once you're on track to healing a different side effect from the disorder. However, if you understand and identify the things you are dealing with (like in exercise thirteen), you'll be able to create a better course of action.

Again, what may work for one person, may not work for another. C-PTSD symptoms are formed from experience, genetics, and your core self. But, the overall approach can be similar.

C-PTSD is a fairly new disorder and is difficult to diagnose, not only because many of the symptoms can overlap with other personality and mood disorders but also because there isn't a lot of research on it. The side effects are presently based on the trauma you've experienced. Even if you're high-functioning and live with the symptoms, that doesn't mean that your side effects aren't encroaching on your life.

Identifying and labeling your symptoms is important because it is much easier to work with them once a light is shined on them. You have an incredible opportunity to overcome the issues when you see what they are.

When you begin the work with your counselor, they may talk to you about relational wounding/healing, somatic level, cognitive level, emotional level, and possible life-skills training.

Relational wounding comes from someone who you have a relationship with. To heal this part of yourself (called relational healing), you'll reverse the damage created by working in an attuned, supportive, and safe environment with reparative experiences[38]. This can happen with your therapist, a trusted friend, or a romantic partner with whom you have a strong foundation.

The somatic level of work will include different kinds of bodywork that can help your nervous system slow down. With this work, you will learn how to retrain and regulate your body's experiences in certain situations. You'll remind your body that the world is safe and you can remain calm. This will be a reversal of response where it will react more appropriately.

Cognitive work will work with your brain to narrate, make sense of, and recall what happened. You will discuss history and memories and form constructive beliefs about yourself, others, and the world. This internalization can include redirecting or rewriting the messaging you hear on any given day within any given situation. The messaging tends to affect your thoughts, feelings, or actions negatively. Alternatively, it

---

[38] Wright LMFT, A. (2022, February 3). *The Multifaceted Causes of C-PTSD, and Ways to Heal*. Psychology Today. https://www.psychologytoday.com/us/blog/making-the-whole-beautiful/202202/the-multifaceted-causes-c-ptsd-and-ways-heal

can also be directed outwardly if you feel you cannot protect yourself outside your created bubble.

Your underline_emotional work_underline will deal with emotional regulation, expressions, reconnecting, relearning, or learning how to identify emotions in your body.

Learning life skills can include personal care habits, developing a fulfilling career, wise money management, developing healthy self-supporting habits, and other logistical skills that contribute to a better quality of life.

When the recording of your trauma plays and replays, chances are it tells you some lie about how you are unlovable, unlikeable, incapable, etc. When humans don't like or care about themselves, they do not try to function at a higher level. Instead, they work on the level they think they deserve. This level can include not taking regular showers, not educating yourself in ways that help challenge your mind, not taking care of your household, etc.

The important thing to remember through all the treatment work is that you deserve to be happy. Some of the work will be more difficult than others. Certain issues can last much longer, and there will be times when you may want to give up. But don't. Keep going. No matter how painful this therapy is, it only lasts a short time (even though it may seem to drag on). By putting yourself in uncomfortable mental and emotional spaces for brief periods, you're helping your present- and future-self gain control of the terrible situation you were placed in.

Stages of Healing From Childhood Trauma

Though you will not have a set direction on your path toward healing, there are general stages you will pass over on the journey. The treatment plan you and your mental health professional enact will change for various reasons. Some determiners could be your family structure, whether your childhood offenders are still in your life if you're able to recall events, or how your current life is unfolding.

Susan Yoon, Ph.D[39], Associate Professor at the College of Social Work, The Ohio State University, discusses C-PTSD in this manner:

> "It is important to note that the process of healing looks different for everyone. Yet, one of the very first steps in healing and recovery includes understanding the trauma one experienced. A comprehensive and thorough assessment of traumatic experiences, such as the type, duration, frequency, and severity of the

---

[39] *Yoon, Susan, Ph.D. | College of Social Work- The Ohio State University.* (n.d.). The Ohio State University. Retrieved July 27, 2022, from https://csw.osu.edu/about/faculty-staff/faculty-directory/yoon-susan-phd/

trauma, is critical as it can inform strategies to heal from trauma.

Other steps in the process of healing may include reaching out to trusted family and friends, seeking professional help from mental health professionals, building trust, gaining support from others, receiving services, participating in treatment/therapy, building a healthy self-image, and practicing self-care."

As Dr. Yoon describes, understanding your experience, the disorder, and accepting that help are the primary ways to begin your process of reworking the narrative built by your trauma.

Three of the stages you might experience are:

Getting Real

Finding strength within honesty is probably your biggest step in this process. It usually is the first point as well. If you know something isn't right with how your brain works, your reactions, or you just feel unhappy, self-reflection is the best way to look at your life. If you find that there are things you believe have harmed you and have history-based effects, then you can make a safe place for yourself to begin that on your road to honesty.

Therapy and therapists should never tell you what you want to hear—if they do, you'll never learn how to be honest with yourself. Their job, along with the professional expertise of psychiatry, is to hold the mirror up for you and expose the places that need to heal.

This experience is part of the healing process but isn't always easy to go through. There will be times when you reject what the therapist is saying or even feel you're provoked negatively. You may even start to think that you want to quit therapy.

When this discomfort starts to push through, it's important to note. It's also crucial to realize that the reason you're becoming provoked by your therapy sessions or therapist's words isn't that they aren't working, but because they are[40].

If you instantly react to something your counselor says instead of mulling it over for a bit, that is a sign of them hitting a nerve. The nerve can be hiding something you believe is embarrassing about your past, or it can be something that has to do with your trauma. The reason may even be different each time you react, but if you are honest with yourself, you can start to pull apart where the sensitivity is coming from[41].

The best place you can come from is to understand that being honest with yourself will help you move through life more easily (and release a lot of anxiety). It will also help you stay

[40] ChoosingTherapy.com. (2022, May 10). *Healing From Childhood Trauma: The Process & Effective Therapy Options*. Choosing Therapy. https://www.choosingtherapy.com/healing-from-childhood-trauma/
[41] ChoosingTherapy.com. (2022, May 10). *Healing From Childhood Trauma: The Process & Effective Therapy Options*. Choosing Therapy. https://www.choosingtherapy.com/healing-from-childhood-trauma/

in check with your actions, words, emotions, etc. You don't have to like what other people say, but thinking about something before you react to it will help you decide what is honest and what is just someone else's opinion.

Exercise Fourteen—Where in Your Life Can You Get Real with Yourself?

Instructions: The echoes of trauma are long and cast shadows over your life until you start to be honest with yourself. Take the list below and write one thing (or many) about your past, actions, behaviors, emotions, etc., where you believe you avoid an honest discourse. Talk with your therapist about these statements and journal how it feels after you say the claims out loud.

For example: I was abused in my childhood. Because of it, I have trouble connecting to people healthily. I don't know how to be in an intimate relationship, so I focus on the instant gratification of casual sex.

_____

_____

_____

_____

_____

_____

_____

_____

_____

_____

_____

_____

_____

_____

_____

_____

_____

_____

_____

_____

_____

_____

_____

_____

Acceptance

After you've chosen to be honest with yourself and accept other people's (especially those who are there to support and love you) input about your issues, behaviors, etc., you'll have to jump into the pool of acceptance.

This stage is not an easy one to dig into.

In fact, long after you're on your healing journey, some of the things you went through may still seem so far from reality that it is hard to believe they happened to you.

But, they did happen.

Accepting the fact that you've been abused, neglected, and traumatized takes an enormous amount of courage. It also includes the idea that certain people in your life who were supposed to protect you did not. They may have even been the ones who inflicted the trauma on you. Despite the intentional or unintentional harm brought to you by these people, your life and person were forever altered by their actions.

Your mom may love you, but that doesn't mean she knows how to be a good mom. She may have grown up in a terrible environment that did not help her develop the maternal, nurturing emotions that a child needs to survive in a healthy world. Instead, you may have been subjected to her ignorance by neglect. You may love your mom, but that doesn't mean she took good care of you. It also doesn't mean that you were given the life you deserved.

Love and attachment to a parent or caregiver can make things difficult to untangle. How can someone love and neglect you? How can your caretaker forget to feed you?

There are many variables here that make acceptance hard to grasp. But, know that just because you are pointing out the reality of a situation doesn't mean that you don't love the person you are talking about. Instead, look at it as making real claims from an observational standpoint[42].

If you weren't fed on a regular basis. Say it. If your caregivers choose relationships over you. Explain that observation. If one or both of your parents didn't know how to be a parent, it would affect you.

When you accept these parts of your life, you are opening yourself up to growth and giving yourself the gift of healing. So many people are too afraid to relay their objective reality because they worry about what that will mean about them and the people who harmed them. Don't let fear of what might happen or what would happen if you admit the truth stop you from accepting your reality.

If you have C-PTSD, you've gone through a prolonged period of trauma. If it was a prolonged period, you're more likely than not to have been abused or neglected by a caregiver.

Acceptance doesn't mean that you won't have these people in your life or that they will suddenly admit to what happened. It does mean that you are taking agency in your life and making the right changes to move toward a better life and well-being.

---

[42] ChoosingTherapy.com. (2022, May 10). *Healing From Childhood Trauma: The Process & Effective Therapy Options*. Choosing Therapy. https://www.choosingtherapy.com/healing-from-childhood-trauma/

Exercise Fifteen—What Do You Have To Accept?

Instructions: As stated above, coming to terms with certain things, especially traumatic things, will leave a footprint on certain parts of your psyche, emotions, feelings, and physicality. What are the things you have to accept in order to take this step? What are some items you're afraid to touch because they are too hard to admit? Write down something or many things and rework them into phrases of acceptance.

For example: My grandfather was an abusive alcoholic. He took his anger out on his family, which turned the family into a toxic environment. This toxicity created children who wouldn't know how to parent their kids and perpetuated the abusive and neglectful features into my childhood.

_____

_____

_____

_____

_____

_____

_____

_____

_____

_____

_____

_____

_____

_____

_____

_____

_____

_____

_____

_____

_____

_____

_____

Growth focus

There are many difficult parts of coping with and healing C-PTSD. One of the healing effects will be that many people don't understand what you are doing. They may be so confused and try to talk you out of therapy, the plan you set for yourself, or they may even deny it happens.

These moments are going to test you greatly.

Sometimes, someone you love and believe supports you will have you questioning your judgment and experiences. They may love and support you, but they may not understand what you're going through because they never went through it themselves.

Another possibility is that they don't understand what you're doing for yourself because they wouldn't do it for themselves (at least not yet). When people cannot relate to something, there is a tendency to "poo-poo" it. That doesn't mean it's wrong for you—it isn't right for them at their place.

Listen to your gut when these moments happen (because they will, sadly). Above all else, follow your instincts and keep moving forward. You aren't healing yourself for other people's approval, and you're healing yourself for yourself because you deserve it.

Self-growth takes focus, self-reflection, and accountability. Healing your C-PTSD is no different than studying for a test or preparing your body for a physical contest. It all takes a lot of work, training, and determination[43].

This stage will involve you gathering resources, lowering your ego, and giving in to some temporary discomfort. In this phase, you'll accept shortcomings, build a support group (friends and professionals), and seek additional insurance and financial help (if need be). You will have to ask for help and be ready to accept it. You'll learn new skills and expand your understanding of how discomfort and growth work together.

Think about your mental, physical, and emotional health as a

---

[43] ChoosingTherapy.com. (2022, May 10). *Healing From Childhood Trauma: The Process & Effective Therapy Options*. Choosing Therapy. https://www.choosingtherapy.com/healing-from-childhood-trauma/

garden. If it is not properly cared for, attended to, and watered, the plants wither and die. Then you get unwanted infestations.

But, when you nourish the garden with self-care, healthy food, and physical activity, your brain, heart, and body blossom in unique ways.

Tending to your mental health is not an easy task because it is so uncomfortable. It's more uncomplicated to let life pull you by the strings and move through the waves while stuffing all your issues below the surface.

But, when you do that, you'll be prone to anxiety, depression, blow-ups, substance abuse, and more.

When you focus on your growth and healing plan, you will see these positive life changes start to bloom around you:

- Improved self-esteem.

- Improved understanding of what you bring to personal and work relationships.

- New goals and interests.

- Renewed objectives and interests.

- New life choices that focus on a healthier life.

- Plans for a better future.

- Healed relationships with healthy friends and family.

- New relationships that are respectful, kind, and caring[44].

"Unfortunately, there is no magic number when it comes to the length of time it takes for an individual to heal from childhood trauma. Some people, especially young children who tend to show greater resilience, bounce back quickly from adversity. For others, healing is a lifelong journey. Taken together, it is important to view healing as a process rather than as an outcome or final product. Recovery and healing can take time, but it is certainly possible[45]."

While it is hard to determine what timeframe it will take to start feeling better, know that with every stage you go through, you're a little closer to a healthier and happier life.

Exercise Sixteen—Where Would You Like To See Yourself?

Instructions: Think about growth focus and what your main goal is. Where do you want to see yourself in six months? Take this time to have a heart-to-heart with yourself. Your six-month goal can be therapy-, career-, personal-, or socially-

[44] ChoosingTherapy.com. (2022, May 10). *Healing From Childhood Trauma: The Process & Effective Therapy Options.* Choosing Therapy. https://www.choosingtherapy.com/healing-from-childhood-trauma/

[45] *Yoon, Susan, Ph.D. | College of Social Work- The Ohio State University.* (n.d.). The Ohio State University. Retrieved July 27, 2022, from https://csw.osu.edu/about/faculty-staff/faculty-directory/yoon-susan-phd/

related. When the thoughts come into your head that say, "I can't do this," or "I always wanted to, but-," ignore them. Those phrases will not be helpful with this exercise. You can write down one, six, fifty, etc., and don't stop until you feel like you have your goals out of you (be realistic as well) or until your gut tells you to stop.

Getting these goals and ideas out can give you a reason you want to focus. Your goals and plans may change over time, but you'll learn how to be more flexible with that idea as you go through more therapy and understand yourself better.

For example: I want to figure out how I can go back to college to pursue a new career in music.

_____

_____

_____

_____

_____

_____

_____

_____

_____

_____

_____

_____

_____

_____

_____

_____

_____

_____

_____

_____

_____

_____

_____

_____

_____

Conclusion

This section covered the profound effect healing and reframing your C-PTSD burden can have on your life. This section discussed how to heal, treatment plans, and different stages of healing your C-PTSD.

While there is no set plan or timeframe for healing, the work you put in will match the changes in your life you experience. Though there are general stages of honesty, acceptance, and growth, the focus is usually the first three on the road to your recovery.

Everything else will depend on genetics, experiences, and how your mind works with the therapy plan you've created.

In the next section, you'll learn about long-term healing plans, how to accept and change your inner dialogue, stop intrusive thoughts, and find ways to look at things positively.

Long Term Healing

A Commitment to Replacing Old Habits with New habits

Introduction

Complex PTSD is a tricky business; to be frank, it's not fair. It's not your fault that you were traumatized. Before your brain gives you the recording that you did something wrong to encourage the abuse, i.e., you weren't listening; you were dressed a certain way; you should have said something differently; no one deserves any type of abuse, no matter what you do. No one. And you did not deserve it. Nor was it your fault.

This phrase—*it's not my fault, I didn't ask for it*—is one you should get used to saying to yourself. Verbal and internal reminders of this message will help you keep going when you feel like giving up.

Those who say it is the deck you were dealt with are sorely generalizing your experience. However unfortunate, you now get to deal with the consequences of your trauma. There will be moments in your recovery when you will start to find that you like yourself and that you like yourself just the way you are.

When you accept yourself just as you are, it can send some confusing signals.

There will be times when you are comfortable with who you are. Then there will be times when you may think, "Who would I be without my trauma?" Finally, you'll have other thoughts, "It's my trauma that made me who I am today."

The message can wax and wane for many years. The ups and downs you experience can be a paradox wrapped in an enigma that will eventually let you let go of the feelings and ideas quickly because many thoughts and emotions are no longer helpful to you.

Long-term healing is a commitment to yourself. You will begin replacing old habits with new ones. These new habits will be healthy, refreshing, and surprising. You may be shunning away from meat when you've been a lifelong lover of a carnivorous diet. You may realize that your personal attachments in your traumatized state are no longer healthy for your lifestyle. You may discover that you want to play the drums. Many things will change, but at your core, you will still be you.

And that is where healing is beautiful. You will discover your whole self exactly how you were meant to be, despite anything that happened to you. And every step you take in the healing process will make you that much stronger.

Accepting Change and Discomfort

Every stage you go through will lay new challenges on your shoulders. Many times these challenges will come as a surprise to you. In conjunction with the surprise challenges, you'll have to think you know how to manage the new phase when you have to strengthen the tools in your belt.

By this point in therapy, you may have a few different feelings—you may decide that it seems as though you're always unhappy, so you might be thinking about quitting. You may realize that you hate how you feel and want it to stop but know it's happening for a reason. Or, you can accept the reality of change and embrace the discomfort. (Or a host of other things, there is no "right" way to experience the difference, but the ideas above are common ones.)

When you embrace the comfort, you'll understand that you're going to feel a certain way "for now." This feeling doesn't mean you'll be feeling this way daily. Instead, it will ebb and flow throughout your days until you barely recognize the discomfort is there.

If you dislike how you are feeling, that's normal. It's called discomfort for a reason. You're in new territory, and any unique experience makes anyone uncomfortable. But, your discomfort over building new habits is a little more intense than just roller-skating for the first time or starting a new job. Your unease is a constant reminder that you are healing and rebuilding your life differently.

The difficulty comes when you try to balance your present life while rehashing past moments. There will be moments when it gets overwhelming, which is where the "always unhappy" feeling sets in. This will be the juncture where you will start thinking about quitting the healing process—and while only you know what is best for you—try not to give it up. You are very close to a breakthrough if you're tired, emotional, and just had enough.

Remember, your brain was built to protect you—if it thinks you are harming yourself, it will try to get you to revert to the way you were. Not because your brain wants you to suffer, but because it hasn't been developed to be resilient due to the trauma.

Talk to your mental health provider if you feel like you need a break and seriously cannot go on. They are your partner on this journey and understand the ins and outs of the process more than anyone else.

Struggling against the discomfort will give you the feeling of walking against the current in a river. It is going to add to your pain and heighten things more than they might have to be. Now, there are situations where the chemicals in your brain will cause this struggle, and the more you heal, the more you realize it's a chemical imbalance than the efforts you are taking.

Chemical imbalances can be fixed with medication. The world is in a good place with these medicines, and instead of masking your feelings and thoughts, they help your emotions and ideas cut through the fog of chemicals so you can get to the heart of the matter.

Medication may not be for everyone and should not be forced on you by any provider. However, with C-PTSD, mediation can help make all the difference in your recovery.

How to Function in Daily Life with All the "Healing" Happening

Healing is a messy business, but just because you're in the process of recovering doesn't mean that the world will stop for you. Instead, you'll have to juggle your mental health with a career, friends, family, and personal life. Depending on your situation, you may have to make a few changes.

While that idea may sound unsettling, know that the changes are going to help inspire a more productive healing process.

Your changes don't have to be huge, but even making sure that you have fifteen minutes for yourself each day to reflect or journal is going to play a big part in your recovery. Other choices will play a role in how you take care of yourself and what your long-term healing will look like.

When you begin your daily tasks, anxiety, shame, and other emotions may bob to the surface at unfortunate times. Taking daily time out for yourself (the fifteen minutes, as mentioned earlier) will help you remain grounded and ease any uncomfortable feelings.

Below are a few exercises you can try to help yourself stay or get to a calm place of mind when things seem to be spiraling out of control. If these exercises don't feel comfortable at first, that is normal.

Exercise Seventeen—Keywords for Mindfulness

Instructions: If you'd like to find some of your exercises, use keywords like "mindful," "meditation," "calm," "balanced," "ease," and "peace." You can write other helpful keywords in the blank space below that will fit your lifestyle, beliefs, and personality.

Use the keywords you've come up with to search online, a local bookstore, and libraries to find other resources to help you center yourself when you're in a tornado of feelings. You can try audio, visual, and literature. Work with your strengths, what keeps your interests, and find the best approach for you, your beliefs, and your lifestyle.

Dr. Alice Boyes[46], author, and psychology researcher focusing on personality and social changes, developed a list of fifty strategies to beat anxiety. Her article "50 Strategies to Beat Anxiety" was published on Psychology Today's website and has some excellent advice.

Exercise Eighteen—Mindfulness Tools (by Dr. Alice Boyes[47])

1. Take a slow breath. Continue slow breathing for three minutes.

2. Drop your shoulders and do a gentle neck roll.

3. Read aloud your emotions, e.g., "I feel angry and worried right now."

4. Massage your hand, which will activate oxytocin.

---

[46] *Alice Boyes Ph.D. About.* (n.d.). Psychology Today. Retrieved July 28, 2022, from https://www.psychologytoday.com/us/contributors/alice-boyes-phd
[47] Boyes Ph.D., A. (2015, March 15). 50 Strategies to Beat Anxiety. Psychology Today. https://www.psychologytoday.com/us/blog/in-practice/201503/50-strategies-beat-anxiety

5. Put something that's out of place in its place. Physical order often helps us feel a sense of mental order.

6. Take a day trip somewhere with natural beauty.

7. Ask yourself, "What's the worst that could happen?" Then, ask yourself, "How would I cope if that happened?" Now, answer those questions.

8. Take a break from actively working on solving a problem and let your mind keep processing the situation in the background.

9. Take a bath.

10. Forgive yourself for not foreseeing a problem that occurred.

11. Throw out something from your bathroom. (The ordering principle again.)

12. Take a break from watching the news or reading newspapers.

13. Make a phone call you've been putting off.

14. Write an email you've been putting off.

15. Take another type of action on something you've been putting off.

16. Throw something out of your fridge.

17. Try guided mindfulness meditation. (Use Google to identify free resources; some good ones are out there.)

18. Take a break from researching a topic you've been over-researching.

19. Cuddle a baby or a pet.

20. If a mistake you've made is bothering you, create an action plan for how you won't repeat it in the future. Write three brief bullet points.

21. Ask yourself if you're jumping to conclusions. For example, if you're worried someone is very annoyed with you, do you know this is the case—or are you jumping to conclusions?

22. Ask yourself if you're catastrophizing, i.e., thinking that something would be a disaster when it might be unpleasant but not necessarily catastrophic.

23. Forgive yourself for not handling a situation in an ideal way, including interpersonal situations. What's the best thing you can do to move forward positively now?

24. If someone else's behavior has triggered anxiety, try accepting that you may never know the whole reason and background behind the person's behavior.

25. Recognize if your anxiety is caused by someone suggesting a change or change of plans. Understand if you tend to react to changes or unexpected events as threats.

26. Accept that there is a gap between your real and ideal selves. (This is the case for pretty much everybody.)

27. Question your social comparisons. For example, is comparing yourself only to the most successful person you know fair or representative?

28. Think about what's going right in your life. Thinking about the positive doesn't always work when you're anxious, but it can help if anxiety has caused your thinking to become lopsided or is obscuring the big picture.

29. Scratch something off your to-do list for the day by getting it done or just deciding not to do that task today.

30. Ask a friend or colleague to tell you about something they've felt nervous about in the past and to tell you what happened.

31. If you're nervous about an upcoming test, try these quick tips for dealing with test anxiety.

32. Do a task 25 percent more slowly than usual. Allow yourself to savor, not rush.

33. Check if you're falling into any of these thinking traps.

34. Try gentle distraction; find something you want to pay attention to. The key to successful use of distraction when you're anxious is to be patient with yourself if you find you're still experiencing intrusive thoughts.

35. Go to a yoga class, or do a couple of yoga poses in the comfort of your home or office.

36. Get a second opinion from someone you trust. Aim to get their real opinion rather than just reassurance seeking.

37. Allow yourself to do things you enjoy, or don't stress yourself out while waiting for your anxious feelings to calm down naturally.

38. Go for a run.

39. Find something on YouTube that makes you laugh out loud.

40. Lightly run one or two fingers over your lips. This will stimulate the parasympathetic fibers in your lips, which will help you feel calmer.

41. Look back on the anxiety-provoking situation you're in from a time in the future, e.g., six months from now.

Does the problem seem smaller when you view it from further away?

42. Imagine how you'd cope if your "worst nightmare" happened, e.g., your partner left you, you got fired, or you developed a health problem. What practical steps would you take? What social support would you use? Mentally confronting your worst fear can be very useful for reducing anxiety.

43. Call or email a friend you haven't talked to in a while.

44. If you imagine a negative outcome to something you're considering doing, try imagining a positive effect.

45. If you rarely back out of commitments and feel overwhelmed by your to-do list, try permitting yourself to say you can no longer do something you've previously agreed to do.

46. Do any two-minute jobs that have been hanging around on your to-do list. It'll help clear your mental space.

47. Jot down three things you worried about in the past that didn't come to pass.

48. Jot down three things you worried about in the past that did occur but weren't nearly as bad as you imagined.

49. Do a form of exercise you haven't done in the last six months.

50. Allow time to pass. Often, the best way to reduce anxiety is to allow time to pass without doing the types of activities that increase anxiety.

Once you read through Dr. Boyle's suggestions, you may notice that many of them are small tasks you can do throughout the day that take very little time. Some of her examples, like massaging your hand to activate oxytocin or jotting down three things you worried about in the past that didn't happen[48], are tasks that will take five minutes or less. If you work at a desk, you don't even have to get up to do them, and these gestures can help you ease your mind while refocusing your emotions back into the present.

Dr. Boyes mentioned the hormone oxytocin. This chemical is generally called the "love" hormone because it is released to help us bond with others and when we hear music, exercise, and touch others.

For a quick brainwork rundown, oxytocin is a hormone produced in the hypothalamus. It is released into the bloodstream via the pituitary gland. The main function of oxytocin is to help with childbirth—it stimulates the muscles

---

[48] Boyes Ph.D., A. (2015, March 15). 50 Strategies to Beat Anxiety. Psychology Today. https://www.psychologytoday.com/us/blog/in-practice/201503/50-strategies-beat-anxiety

of a uterus to contract, boosts the production of prostaglandins, and will help stimulate the milk ducts in breasts to produce milk, creating a closer bond between the mother and newborn.

Oxytocin is also produced in both genders when falling in love. When you become excited about your sexual partner, your brain will release oxytocin into your bloodstream, which gives you the heady feeling of being in love[49].

Crystal Hoshaw, a professional writer and mindfulness expert[50] wrote an article titled "32 Mindfulness Activities to Find Calm at Any Age," published on the *HealthLine* website. This article is reviewed by Dr. Cheryl Crumper, an expert in behavioral medicine, mindfulness, anxiety, depression management, stress reduction, and mind-body medicine[51].

Within Hoshaw's article, she separates mindful activities between adults, teens, anxiety, and children[52]. And while the activities for children are a bit fun (dragon's breath is a common tool in yoga), they haven't been added to the actions below.

---

[49] Watson, S. (2021, July 20). *Oxytocin: The love hormone*. Harvard Health. https://www.health.harvard.edu/mind-and-mood/oxytocin-the-love-hormone

[50] H. (n.d.). *Crystal Hoshaw*. Healthline. Retrieved July 28, 2022, from https://www.healthline.com/authors/crystal-hoshaw

[51] H. (n.d.-a). *Cheryl Crumpler, PhD*. Healthline. Retrieved July 28, 2022, from https://www.healthline.com/reviewers/cheryl-crumpler-phd

[52] Hoshaw, C. (2022, June 22). *32 Mindfulness Activities to Find Calm at Any Age*. Healthline. https://www.healthline.com/health/mind-body/mindfulness-activities

Exercise Nineteen—Mindful Activities to Help Center You

1. **Create a gratitude list**—this activity can help improve your well-being, promote positivity, and help you focus on things you are grateful for. You can add three to five items to your list daily and stay consistent with your gratitude. The common practice is adding to your list when you wake up or just before bed. However, adding them to your lunch hour can also break up your day nicely.

2. **Try walking meditation**—this form of meditation is practiced by walking most often in a straight line or a circle. This exercise can happen almost anywhere—you can do this by walking at work, around the neighborhood, or at the park with your family. The trick is to walk but move through your thoughts. So, basically, you'll be walking your troubles away.

3. **Driving mindfully**—if you like driving, this activity is for you. You can set out for a day trip or drive around your area. This type of meditation has you focus on the weight of your automobile, the texture of the road, the sound of your tires against the concrete, and the shape and feel of the seat against your body. You will then scan your surroundings. Become aware of the other vehicles on the road, the traffic lights, pedestrians, terrain, and the skyline. This practice can also encourage

you to become a better driver—keep your phone, and the radio turned off. Just listen to what you are experiencing presently.

4. **Focus on a single task**—instead of multi-tasking, which you are amazing at, you dial back your focus onto one project. This activity will require you to put all your focus on whatever task you have in front of you.

   For example: when working on the computer, close any tabs that aren't relevant to the project you're working on.

   This exercise will help you free up mental space and give you laser focus.

   To go deeper within this practice, pay attention to:

   • How you breath

   • What your body feels like (how you're standing, your seat, etc.)

   • The sensation of your clothes on your skin

   • How is your posture[53].

5. **Eating mindfully**—when you eat mindfully, you are slowing down the process of how you nourish your

---

[53] ibid.

body. If you turn this into daily practice, you'll realize that you are eating healthier too. But that isn't the primary focus. Instead, you'll take a mindful approach to what you're putting in your mouth, how you are putting it in there, how you are chewing, and making sure to savor, taste, and relax into every bite[54].

To go deeper into this mindful practice, you can:

- Eat with your non-dominant hand (if you write with your right hand, eat with your left).

- Focus on your food's flavors, texture, and smells while eating in silence for the first few moments of your meal.

- Put away your phone, avoid streaming video, and turn off your TV.

6. **Gardening mindfully**—have you connected with nature and the earth in a new way you may not have tried? Start small and understand that if you're new to gardening, your first few plants may die—it happens to all gardeners. You can plant seeds or water flowers. If you are okay with putting your hand in the dirt without gloves, you can play with the soil for a few moments and focus on the sensations. Is the dirt fine or rough?

---

[54] Hoshaw, C. (2022, June 22). *32 Mindfulness Activities to Find Calm at Any Age*. Healthline. https://www.healthline.com/health/mind-body/mindfulness-activities

Is it dry? Is it cool or warm? Process these thoughts and think about how you would be if you were a child playing.

7. **Appreciate music**—everyone likes music in their own way. However, it's a great way to enter into mindfulness while using your favorite music. You can use headphones or new music, but find a space where you won't be interrupted. Pick a song that is a reasonable length and simply kick back and listen to the music. Ask yourself:

- How does your body feel?

- What layers of music can you find (different instruments, harmonies, etc.)

- What is your breath like when you hear different songs?

8. **Moving mindfully**—while cliché, the phrase "dance like nobody's watching" has roots in mindfulness. Moving is a great way to be in your body, let loose, release pent-up energy, and express yourself. You can use music or move in silence. You have to move your body without thinking.

You don't have to make dance moves or worry about your appearance. Just let everything flow, and even if you feel silly at first, if you let yourself get into the motions, you'll realize how great it all feels once you are done.

If your area has dance studios and you are comfortable doing this around people, look around for group-based mindful dance classes.

If you don't want to move to music and don't feel right moving without any purpose, shake everything out in your body. Start with your hands or head and work through all parts, including fingers and toes.

9. **Use puzzles or apps for mindful moments**—puzzles like a jigsaw, crosswords, sudoku, etc., are great ways to sharpen your mind, but they also provide you with a mindfulness practice where you don't think about anything except what is in front of you. You can hone in on specific questions like how your body feels when you get frustrated or when you find a new piece of the puzzle and how your breathing changes throughout the game.

The use of apps varies from person to person. Some people will not mind incorporating technology into their mindfulness practice, whereas others will want to stay away from it. Using apps is not a requirement for mindfulness, but if you fall into the camp and want to try them out, you should.

Many apps focus on mindfulness. You can find guided meditations that last three minutes or three hours. You can find soothing music apps that will guide you into a sense of calmness. You can even find tapping apps to help you find sensitive pressure points that will help release some built-up tension. Use the keyword list you created in Exercise Eighteen to help you find the right apps for you

10. **Scan your body**—this practice is used in meditation and yoga. It helps calm your mind and help you check in with your body by using self-awareness to become in tune with what is happening. The simple practice is to lie down and relax. Then you'll mentally scan your toes, calves, knees, hips, and upward until you reach your head. Hit every part of your body you want to, including the stomach, heart, mind, etc. Check in with each part and feel the sensations—do you have pain or tension in this area? If so, find different ways to help yourself release that physical discomfort.

11. **Box breathing**—this type of breathing has specific instructions where you inhale for a count of three, hold for a count of four, and exhale for a count of four. You can use box breathing when it seems nothing else is working to calm you down (or if you just like it). You're also encouraging focus, concentration, and performance when you breathe in this manner. People

in high-stress careers like nurses, police, US Navy seals, and professional athletes use box breathing[55].

12. **Self-compassion**—anxiety tends to prompt fear, resistance, and negative personal views. Instead of looking at your anxiety as a shortcoming, reframe the idea and use it as a strength—yes, you may have anxiety, but that means you are healing. Or, yes, you have anxiety, but you're going to kickass at whatever you do anyway.

If you find that blame or self-blame for certain actions comes into your head, let that go and remind yourself that you've gone through an ordeal, so while you are healing, you are still learning about yourself, as you are now, so compassion and love will be the best way to let things go[56].

13. **Try some art**—art is a great tool to shut your mind down and let your creativity take over. When you're doing mindful art, it's more about allowing creativity to run its course and not about how perfect everything has to be. Instead, paint, craft, color, draw, doodle, etc., with your emotions and let your thoughts float through your mind.

---

[55] Gotter, A. (2020, June 17). *Box Breathing*. Healthline.
https://www.healthline.com/health/box-breathing
[56] Hoshaw, C. (2022, June 22). *32 Mindfulness Activities to Find Calm at Any Age*. Healthline. https://www.healthline.com/health/mind-body/mindfulness-activities

Not all the exercises listed above are short, and some will take practice, especially to incorporate them into your daily life. Still, once you find the right pattern of mindfulness for you, you may notice that you're trying different variations (of your own making!) to suit your needs at each moment.

Exercise Twenty—Five-Minute Mindful Activities.

Instructions: Try out the five-minute mindful activities when you don't have much time to spare, but feel the need to relax your mind and emotions.

1. **Breathing**—use basic breathing as a straightforward and simple meditation when you need to refocus or when your anxiety threatens to burst out your seams. Set your timer for five minutes so you can know when your time is up and don't have to feel like you have to check the clock continuously.

   a. Step One: sit in a comfortable position (if you're in an environment to lie down and want to, you can).

   b. Step Two: Inhale and observe your breath.

   c. Step Three: Exhale and focus on the breath.

   d. Step Four: Gently bring your focus back to your breath each time your mind wanders away.

   If you're looking to deepen your practice, you can focus

on physical sensations:

- What are your chest and belly doing?

- How does your breath feel in your throat and nostrils?

- The feeling of your body against the floor, bed, or seat.

Use this practice daily; if you have the time, you can go longer than five minutes.

2. **Deep Seeing**—like box breathing, this exercise uses a specific focus on the present moment. It will engage your visual senses and have you tune into your surroundings. Don't forget to set your alarm or timer for five minutes when beginning this practice.

   a. Step One: Select an object that you enjoy. (This can be a colorful vase, a piece of fruit, a plant, etc.)

   b. Step Two: Look at the object and hone in on new elements of this object you haven't seen before. Focus on colors, textures, folds, shapes, and sizes. Look for imperfections.

    c.   <u>Step Three</u>: When your alarm goes off, slowly pull yourself away from the object and take a few moments to recognize how you feel[57].

3. **Deep listening**—this exercise is very similar to the previous exercise of deep seeing. However, in this case, you'll sit and listen to what is happening around you. Listen to sounds close to you, your breath, the humming of an electronic device, a pet scratching itself. Set a timer for five minutes and practice this daily[58].

The exercises mentioned above are not the end-all-be-all ones. If you choose to use any of them, they can provide you with a learning foundation of mindfulness. Don't be alarmed if you feel weird when you first start. Feeling odd, silly, or embarrassed at doing something you haven't done before is a normal reaction.

Pick a few exercises each day and do them for at least three weeks to see if they suit your personality and lifestyle well. If they do not, move on to the next one. Eventually, something will stick, and you'll be able to get into an amazing mindfulness practice.

---

[57] Hoshaw, C. (2022, June 22). *32 Mindfulness Activities to Find Calm at Any Age.* Healthline. https://www.healthline.com/health/mind-body/mindfulness-activities

[58] Hoshaw, C. (2022, June 22). *32 Mindfulness Activities to Find Calm at Any Age.* Healthline. https://www.healthline.com/health/mind-body/mindfulness-activities

Stop Intrusive Thoughts

Intrusive thoughts are a harmful side effect of C-PTSD. These thoughts can keep you up at night, run through your mind in a ruminating cycle, and severely hinder your progress. Intrusive thoughts are sudden, involuntary, and unwanted thoughts that will reinforce the fears you have about yourself and your disorder. These thoughts can be of things that happened during the day or of something that happened thirty years ago.

Each time an intrusive thought pops up, it is shocking and attached to a feeling as if it was happening in the present time. They tend to keep you down on yourself, lower your self-esteem, and usually occur when things are going well—a side effect that keeps you "down."

While these thoughts are far from true, they do have an intense ability to stop you cold and make you question your judgment, actions, feelings, and more.

The amazing news is that you can completely manage or stop intrusive thoughts. And, of course, it will take a little bit of work and some determination on your end.

Below are a few ways and exercises to help you challenge these thoughts.

- **Face your problem**—the most helpful thing you can

do for yourself and your mind against intrusive thoughts is to deal with the issue. As mentioned before, when you face what is going on in your life and psyche, you can control your narrative instead of letting it control you.

When you don't deal with your traumatized issues and emotions, they will eke out in unhealthy ways and cause you to do things you may have never done without C-PTSD.

Complex PTSD has made a few adjustments to your brain, so you are in the phase of getting to know yourself. Don't make it harder and avoid the bigger issues just because they are scary and uncomfortable[59].

- **Separate the rational from the irrational**—many of the thoughts you'll have swarming your mind will be unreasonable. Although, it really won't feel like it. However, these are the moments where positive self-talk and an objective inner voice will help you decipher the rational from the exaggerated.

  Your ability to separate these thoughts will come with time and practice, but you must start somewhere. If you are having issues figuring out what is an irrational idea, think about the facts. What truly happened? How did it

---

[59] Murphy, A. (2022, March 30). *How to Stop Intrusive Thoughts: 8 Effective Ways.* Declutter The Mind. https://declutterthemind.com/blog/how-to-stop-intrusive-thoughts/

really happen? What emotions are attached to this thought? Can you tell why this emotion popped in with the thought?

Irrational thoughts come from insecurity, fear, doubt, and the unknown. When you received the trauma, your brain programmed itself into a new way of working. It is incredibly difficult to reroute your brain patterns—but it is by no means impossible. Little steps toward the right train of thought will rewrite and rewire your brain so you'll have less intrusive thoughts coming into your mind and a thought process that is based on reality.

Exercise Twenty-One—What is a Rational Thought?

Instructions:

1. Write down an intrusive thought, then dissect it.

2. Pull out the authentic pieces from the exaggerated and emotionally-based details.

3. See how your intrusive thoughts respond differently from reality and work to rewrite that narrative.

4. Use the new narrative every time the intrusive thought comes back again.

5. Try this practice on at least six intrusive thoughts to see if it works. If it does, keep up the method whenever

another thought comes to mind.

Example: I was such an ass when I was talking to my group of friends. I laughed too loudly, talked too much, and came across as a pompous know-it-all.

Reality	Exaggeration
My friends love me.	I was too loud.
I was excited to see everyone	I talked too much.
My loud laughing and chatting fear is my insecurity of being the center of attention. Because if too many people notice me, I'll get abused again.	I am a pompous know-it-all.
I am nervous that I said or did the wrong thing because people who abused me always told me it was my fault when they did something to me.	I was an ass.

| I make sure to listen as much as I talk to make sure everyone feels heard and part of the group. | |

Rewriting the narrative: I had a lot of fun with my friends. We laughed and talked together for a long time. It seems like everyone enjoyed themselves.

Your Turn:

Intrusive Thought:

_____

_____

_____

_____

_____

_____

_____

_____

_____

_____

_____

_____

_____

Reality	Exaggeration

Rewrite your Narrative:

_____

_____

_____

_____

_____

_____

_____

_____

_____

_____

Intrusive Thought:

_____

_____

_____

_____

_____

_____

_____

_____

_____

_____

Reality	Exaggeration

Rewrite your Narrative:

_____

_____

_____

_____

_____

_____

_____

_____

_____

_____

Continue this process at least four times to get an idea if this exercise will help redirect your intrusive thoughts.

- **Incorporate more gratitude**—it is easier to focus on the negative than on the positive things in your life, especially when intrusive thoughts come into play. However, using gratitude to erase and rework the intrusive thoughts is a great way to flip negative insecurity into a positive life force[60].

---

[60] Murphy, A. (2022, March 30). *How to Stop Intrusive Thoughts: 8 Effective Ways.* Declutter The Mind. https://declutterthemind.com/blog/how-to-stop-intrusive-thoughts/

Exercise Twenty-Two—Your Gratitude List.

Think about things you are grateful for in your life. Write down a list of ideas below so you can use them during intrusive thoughts. If you have an intrusive thought, you can also use the workspace below to write down things you are grateful for at the moment. Or, you can always carry around a handheld notebook to fill out when the thoughts strike out at you.

_____

_____

_____

_____

_____

_____

_____

_____

_____

_____

_____

_____

_____

_____

_____

_____

_____

_____

Use this list when you cannot think of anything to be grateful for or if you are feeling especially blue because of intrusive thoughts. You can add things to your list daily or only add things when it works for you. Remembering the good things you have in life when your mind is sending you on a negative spiral can really help pull yourself out of the minefield.

- **Flip your script**—the way you look at the world will vastly affect how your mind works. Yes, there are terrible things happening every day to an enormous amount of people, places, creatures, and things—but there are also people, places, creatures and things that are doing good in the world. When you catch yourself feeling low or that you are having some gnarly thoughts about life, flip the script. Turn it into something positive.

This doesn't mean that when you're upset about the whaling industry you change it to "Hey, at least bunnies are fluffy." Instead you can find out what activists are doing to help the whales and to stop poachers from hurting them again.

- **Incorporate healthy habits**—when you have a healthy body, you have a healthy mind, and vice versa. It is vital that you choose healthy habits, even if you have to start small. If you smoke, make the choice to quit. Talk to your doctor about your best options and commit to it. If you have issues with eating, reach out to a PCP, dietician, or nutritionist. If you have issues with insurance, then start researching online for free or low-cost healthy habits you can build into your life. The more you do, the more you're going to want to do[61].

- **Journal, Journal, Journal**—getting your thoughts out of your head will make room for different and more vibrant thoughts to come. They will also give you a chance to see the full thought, which can help you with the visualization and can also show you how rational or irrational the thoughts are. Brain dumps are an amazing tool that can get any anxiety out of your brain and body and help you realize what triggered the anxiety. Once you can label it, you can start coming up with some ideas to manage it.

- **Your thoughts as clouds**—with each thought that passes and doesn't stick, you are making steps forward. Think about your thoughts as clouds and let them float by. There will be ones that try to recycle themselves, but when you find that they've grabbed on, release them back into the sky and let them continue on their way. If you don't give your power to the intrusive thoughts, they will have less motivation to come back and bother you.

---

[61] Murphy, A. (2022, March 30). *How to Stop Intrusive Thoughts: 8 Effective Ways*. Declutter The Mind. https://declutterthemind.com/blog/how-to-stop-intrusive-thoughts/

- Keep your therapy appointments—if you have C-PTSD, you should have a therapist. If you haven't found the right one, keep looking, but continue talking to a counselor while you are on your journey. Complex PTSD isn't a condition that goes away by ignoring it; when you ask for help from someone, you give yourself the biggest gift you can. Talking about your intrusive thoughts and getting your counselor's perspective can provide you with insight and professional opinions on how to best tackle the unpleasant issue[62].

Positive Ways of Dealing with C-PTSD

Healing C-PTSD is a collaborative process between you and the people in your life, including the professionals. While it is natural to feel as though your entire world has shattered, remind yourself that if something is destroyed, it can be built back up—usually better than ever before and exactly how you want it to be.

Before you remember that, the pain, loss, and loneliness of C-PTSD can be overwhelming. Your thoughts and emotions are a swirling mess that you may not understand. Trauma-induced fits of negative feelings will play tricks on your brain,

---

[62] Murphy, A. (2022, March 30). *How to Stop Intrusive Thoughts: 8 Effective Ways.* Declutter The Mind. https://declutterthemind.com/blog/how-to-stop-intrusive-thoughts/

and until you can disconnect from those, your reactions to the intrusive thoughts and other side effects of C-PTSD will be very unhealthy for you, and you don't deserve that.

Through your recovery, you're going to come across a lot of tools that can help you. Positive ways of dealing with and managing C-PTSD can keep you going when you are at a loss for words and feeling less than hopeful.

Exercise Twenty-Three—Positive Ways to Deal

- **Start small.** Set realistic goals that are attainable within a few hours or days. Think about where you'd like to be tomorrow and what things you can do when you get there.

- **Manage your larger tasks into modest chunks.** Instead of tackling everything at once, there is no need to add extra pressure to yourself. Instead, remember that you already have enough tension and anxiety writhing through your body—give yourself a break and let your projects unfold slowly without shooting yourself in the good[63].

- **Find social support and avoid isolation.** Now, more than ever, you'll need help feeling loved. With C-PTSD, there will be times when it is painful to love yourself.

---

[63] *10 Positive Ways of Dealing with PTSD | HealthyPlace.* (2021, December 17). The Healthy Place. https://www.healthyplace.com/ptsd-and-stress-disorders/ptsd/10-positive-ways-of-dealing-with-ptsd

That is when you will need the most support from outside sources—even if you want to crawl under your blanket and hibernate. You have C-PTSD because you were abused and neglected, which you did not deserve. Be the caretaker you never had and reach out to someone that can give you the support you need right when you need it most.

- **Build your life skills, including communicative and problem-solving ones.** Complex PTSD will interfere with your ability to communicate with others and solve problems. You may find yourself thinking that something can't be done because it appears like you've hit a roadblock, but instead, you'll have to train yourself to know that there are always alternative options. Work with your counselor or therapists to help rebuild your communication center and learn how resilient you are.

- **Workout.** Each day exercise, even if it is just a ten to fifteen-minute routine to start with. Give yourself mild activity that can help increase your well-being and reduce stress.

- **Use relaxation techniques to decrease hyperarousal when you're having a C-PTSD stress-induced moment.** Intrusive thoughts will come up when you least expect them, but they can occur anytime. If they happen to you when you're already feeling low, they will be able to tack onto your insecurity even quicker.

They will also lash out more harshly if you've been working to manage them. But they are not in control. Once you remember that you have tools to help you through these negative times, you'll be able to implement them quickly, which can get your mind and emotions back into the right frame of thought—even if you're still feeling a little shaky.

You can use yoga, breathing, exercise, walking, reading, meditation, or a host of other tranquil activities.

- **Find a comforting situation**. Use people or places to help you find comfort when you need it. Start with one person or a small place where you feel safe, and then connect with that person in your safe place. By taking action against your discomfort, you will have an effective way to deal with any C-PTSD side effects.

- **Have fun**. Reintroduce joy and passion into your life. Be creative, play games, and do things that make you laugh. While placing yourself in these moments of happiness may feel weird, you'll feel refreshed and rejuvenated at the end. It is essential for your well-being that you can identify things to bring a little delight into your world for a short time.

- **Look internally for new strengths.** When you have C-PTSD, finding the positive moments of your recovery will give you a refreshed view of the process, help you reengage if you've faltered, and find good in your life for your health[64].

- **Make plans for the future.** When you are intentional with your future, you are showing yourself hope. The traumatized part of you can take a long time to heal itself on its own. But when you plan for the future, something simple—journaling, scrapbooking—and recording your thoughts, you will bring more meaningfulness into your life: use quotes, images, ideas, and more to inspire you. The more you inspire yourself, the more you want to keep going.

Your C-PTSD recovery is an important time to be patient. Healing is not a race but a marathon. Using positive methods and mental health tools to move through the side effects will put you into a place of empowerment and help you move forward every day.

---

[64] *10 Positive Ways of Dealing with PTSD | HealthyPlace.* (2021, December 17). The Healthy Place. https://www.healthyplace.com/ptsd-and-stress-disorders/ptsd/10-positive-ways-of-dealing-with-ptsd

Steps to Healing Childhood Trauma as an Adult

Trauma affects your body, mind, and emotions on many levels. As an adult, you may have reactions you don't understand or believe you're behaving in a way that contradicts your personality. You may live in a lot of confusion.

Complex PTSD will affect your life until you start to process the trauma. Each stage will give you a new level of trauma, and it is always helpful to start on the narrow path and work out toward the wider issues.

Dr. Andrea Brandt[65], and contributor to Psychology Today, developed a nine-step healing process regarding trauma. See her suggestions in the exercise below.

Brant states, "an exercise for processing trauma includes steps such as grounding it, recalling it, naming it, and sharing it[66]."

In her article, "9 Steps to Healing Childhood Trauma as an Adult," Dr. Brant explains that:

---

[65] Psychology Today, P. (n.d.). *Andrea Brandt Ph.D. M.F.T.* Psychology Today. Retrieved July 29, 2022, from https://www.psychologytoday.com/us/contributors/andrea-brandt-phd-mft

[66] Brandt Ph.D. M.F.T., A. (2018, April 2). *9 Steps to Healing Childhood Trauma as an Adult*. Psychology Today. https://www.psychologytoday.com/us/blog/mindful-anger/201804/9-steps-healing-childhood-trauma-adult

"Trauma generates emotions, and unless we process these emotions at the time the trauma occurs, they become stuck in our mind and body. Instead of healing from the wounding event, the trauma stays in our body as energy in our unconscious, affecting our life until we uncover it and process it out. The healthy flow and processing of distressing emotions, such as anger, sadness, shame, and fear, is essential to healing from childhood trauma as an adult[67]."

In the United States, a social stigma comes with crying, anger, fear, and distress. These feelings are looked upon as weakness, and when we, as humans, encounter them and feel them, that means something terrible about our personality. This stigma attacks who we are at our core, which doesn't allow for healthy processing of traumatic events and experiences.

Childhood is an age of egocentrism.

When things are done in our childhood, such as not being taken care of, being neglected, we are abused, we automatically turn those thoughts onto ourselves and blame our actions, words, feelings, and thoughts as the reason why the trauma happened to us.

As we age and do not process the trauma until we take agency over it—when you grow up in an abusive household, you

---

[67] ibid.

cannot absorb the abuse until you leave that environment. Chances are because that abuse is what you've grown up with, you find a relationship that meets the needs of your comfort level. This action will keep you in the abused state until you decide it is time to stop. When you make that choice for yourself, you are creating personal agency.

However, just because you now have agency doesn't mean that your wounds from the trauma automatically go away. To release these trauma-induced habits, you have to process and heal.

The damage from your childhood will be buried under years of other ways you've tormented yourself in self-deprecation because you chose not to deal with your core issues and instead may have developed a hoard of other unhealthy habits as you tried to plug up the dam of unpleasant side effects of C-PTSD.

Continued in her article, Dr. Brant explains

> "To heal from childhood trauma, we have to complete the process that should have begun decades ago, when the wounding incident happened. I developed this exercise based on my decades of experience helping patients heal from childhood emotional wounds[68]."

---

[68] Brandt, A. (2017). *Mindful Aging: Embracing Your Life After 50 to Find Fulfillment, Purpose, and Joy*. PESI Publishing & Media.

Exercise Twenty-Four—Bringing Up Old Wounds

The next exercises come from the same article and are initially suggested in small doses. Preferably do these exercises with a therapist or counselor present. Before starting this exercise, it is good to print out a list of emotions that you may experience. This list will help name and connect emotions while feeling them, which is part of the process. It is merely a cheat sheet if you cannot place something while going through each step.

Step One: Ground It.

To work, you must be in the present. Focus your body and mind in the here and now.

- Find a place where you won't be disturbed.

- Find a comfortable sitting position.

- Deeply inhale several times[69].

- Bring your awareness to your body.

- Squeeze the muscles in your arms, legs, stomach, etc. (Do this one area at a time.)

---

[69] Brandt Ph.D. M.F.T., A. (2018, April 2). *9 Steps to Healing Childhood Trauma as an Adult*. Psychology Today. https://www.psychologytoday.com/us/blog/mindful-anger/201804/9-steps-healing-childhood-trauma-adult

- Release the muscles and feel how heavy each part of your body is as you relax the targeted area.

- Connect to the ground underneath you.

- Visualize a stream of energy tracing straight from your tailbone toward the earth's core.

- After you feel centered, go to step two.

Step Two: Recall it.

- Think of a situation where you've been upset.

- Look at the circumstance; what part provoked a mild to strong emotional reaction? (If you are emotionally numb right now, focus on the instances that should have provoked a reaction.)

- Go over the details of what happened.

- Revisit the event. Imagine you are there in that time and place.

- Experience it again and use all your senses.

- When your emotions percolate, move on to step three.

Step Three: Sense it.

- Continue your deep breathing.

- Spend a moment relaxing in the quiet.

- Mentally scan your body. Target any sensations.

- Your emotions will bubble and stir inside of you.

- Search for physical responses, i.e., burning, tightness, tingling, etc. Each sensation is data. You will need to understand the past moment you are experiencing.

- Silently describe your sensations and be as detailed as you can.

- Explore all physical reactions, then move on to step four.

Step Four: Name It.

- Attach an emotion with each sensation you feel. For example, do you think it is anxiety if you feel tightness in your chest? Can you feel a burst of heat through your body? Is it anger?

- Use your list to help you recognize the subtle distinctions between emotions.

- Name these emotions. This step will give you a better understanding and a richer knowledge of yourself.

- When you've named all emotions, go on to step five[70].

Step Five: Love It.

- Go through each emotion, touching each one as you say it.

- When you feel each emotion, tell that feeling, "I love myself for feeling {INSERT FEELING HERE}." Whether you love it at the time or are uncomfortable, you want to push it away, and it doesn't matter. Say it anyway. Being mindful means accepting all feelings and emotions. You'll need to embrace what it means to be a human and love yourself.

- After you express love for each emotion, move on to step six.

Step Six: Feel it. Experience it.

- Sit with your emotions. Experience each sensation. Let these sensations move throughout your body without changing, hiding, or pushing them away.

- Observe your emotions.

- Accept and welcome the discomfort—have tea with it.

---

[70] Brandt Ph.D. M.F.T., A. (2018, April 2). *9 Steps to Healing Childhood Trauma as an Adult*. Psychology Today. https://www.psychologytoday.com/us/blog/mindful-anger/201804/9-steps-healing-childhood-trauma-adult

- Remind yourself that the uncomfortable sensation will be gone soon. Know that it will help you heal.

- If you feel you need to punch something or yell—punch the air, yell into a pillow. Let your body respond in the way it needs to. Productively expressing your emotions is vital to moving through the recovery process.

- Move on to step seven when you've fully felt your emotions for the day.

Step Seven: Receive its Wisdom and Message.

- Investigate the message your emotions are sending you. Do they connect with one or more experiences you've had? Do they help you root yourself in the trauma or limit a belief about yourself? At first, you might think that you aren't getting anything.

- Ask yourself: "Does this emotion or sensation have something to say? What is it trying to tell me?

- If you cannot find the message in the sensation, try journaling for ten minutes. Use a "Free Writing" tool to transfer all your thoughts down to paper without filtering them. Don't stop for the full ten minutes so you can review what wisdom your emotions are trying to display to you.

- When you believe you've received the information you

were supposed to, move on to step eight.

Step Eight: Share It.

- While this step is optional at first, as you become more comfortable with your emotions and reflections, you'll find that you have an easier time discussing your findings with other people.

- When you are comfortable, share your observations with another person. If you are uncomfortable with this, write them down so you can share them yourself.

- Describe what happened, how you reacted, and how you see it now.

- Writing and talking about your situation is an important part of healing[71].

- You can write letters to those who have hurt you, you don't have to have any intention of sending them, but it is an effective practice to move through emotion and learn to let go.

- Move on to step nine when you've shared your reflections with yourself or with another person.

---

[71] Brandt Ph.D. M.F.T., A. (2018, April 2). *9 Steps to Healing Childhood Trauma as an Adult*. Psychology Today. https://www.psychologytoday.com/us/blog/mindful-anger/201804/9-steps-healing-childhood-trauma-adult

Step Nine: Let it Go.

- Visualize the trauma as energy. Imagine it leaving your body. You can perform a ritual of physical release, such as burning the letter you wrote (in a safe space) or throwing away an object of the trauma.

- Borrow rituals from different spiritual places.

- Let the pain go[72].

This process, while uncomfortable at first, will be very rewarding. The energy you spend on your trauma will be released, and you'll be able to build the life you want and deserve. You will have a more positive outlook on the world and spread your healing energy to the rest of those you care most deeply about.

Conclusion

Section four covers how to heal deep childhood trauma and commit to a long-term healing plan. Each step you take toward recovery is a step in the right direction. Even when you walk away from the path because it is too painful or

---

[72] Brandt Ph.D. M.F.T., A. (2018, April 2). *9 Steps to Healing Childhood Trauma as an Adult*. Psychology Today. https://www.psychologytoday.com/us/blog/mindful-anger/201804/9-steps-healing-childhood-trauma-adult

because life has just taken over and you cannot focus on both, know that your way will always be waiting for you.

You are never too old or too young to take on new growth. You deserve to be happy, whole and supported. You deserve to love yourself.

Wrapping up

This workbook is only one small part of your journey in your recovery. You are going to have times when you feel fantastic and times when you feel very low. Any way you feel, keep going.

The burden of C-PTSD is not yours to bear. You didn't ask for it. You didn't deserve it. You can take your power back and not let those who harmed you have that agency any longer.

Once you discover that your abuser(s) don't control your narrative, the grating parts of your life fall away. Now you control your actions, words, and choices.

"No one can make you feel inferior without your consent."

~ Eleanor Roosevelt.

You deserve to have that for yourself.

Never be alone when working through C-PTSD. Even if you

only have your therapist at first, that is enough support for you. At the end of this book are other resources that can guide you. There are helplines and books to teach you more about your brain and why it works the way it does.

You are strong, worthy, and resilient. You can do this.

You are amazing.

Thank You

Before you leave, I'd just like to say, thank you so much for purchasing my book.

I spent many days and nights working on this book so I could finally put this in your hands.

So, before you leave, I'd like to ask you a small favor.

Would you please consider posting a review on the platform? Your reviews are one of the best ways to support indie authors like me, and every review counts.

Your feedback will allow me to continue writing books just like this one, so let me know if you enjoyed it and why. I read every review and I would love to hear from you. Simply scan this QR code below to leave a review.

Sources

10 Positive Ways of Dealing with PTSD | HealthyPlace. (2021, December 17). The Healthy Place. https://www.healthyplace.com/ptsd-and-stress-disorders/ptsd/10-positive-ways-of-dealing-with-ptsd

A. (2013, May 3). Self-sabotage Worksheet. EFT Masters Worldwide. https://eftmastersworldwide.com/self-sabotage-worksheet/

Alice Boyes Ph.D. About. (n.d.). Psychology Today. Retrieved July 28, 2022, from https://www.psychologytoday.com/us/contributors/alice-boyes-phd

APA Dictionary of Psychology. (n.d.). Https://Dictionary.Apa.Org. Retrieved July 15, 2022, from https://dictionary.apa.org/mindfulness

Banks, K., Newman, E., & Saleem, J. (2015). An Overview of the Research on Mindfulness-Based Interventions for Treating Symptoms of Posttraumatic Stress Disorder: A Systematic Review. Journal of Clinical Psychology, 71(10), 935–963. https://doi.org/10.1002/jclp.22200

Bilodeau, K. (2021, October 1). Managing intrusive thoughts. Harvard Health. https://www.health.harvard.edu/mind-and-mood/managing-intrusive-thoughts

Boyes Ph.D., A. (2015, March 15). 50 Strategies to Beat Anxiety. Psychology Today. https://www.psychologytoday.com/us/blog/in-practice/201503/50-strategies-beat-anxiety

Brandt, A. (2017). Mindful Aging: Embracing Your Life After 50 to Find Fulfillment, Purpose, and Joy. PESI Publishing & Media.

Brandt Ph.D. M.F.T., A. (2018, April 2). 9 Steps to Healing Childhood Trauma as an Adult. Psychology Today. https://www.psychologytoday.com/us/blog/mindful-anger/201804/9-steps-healing-childhood-trauma-adult

Brickel, R. E., MA. (2018, October 24). How to Heal Trauma By Understanding Your Attachment Style. Brickel and Associates LLC. https://brickelandassociates.com/understand-attachment-style-heal-trauma/#:%7E:text=Here%20is%20a%20brief%20list%20of%20the%20four,3%20Anxious%2FInsecure%20%E2%80%93%20preoccupied%204%20Disorganized%20%E2%80%93%20unresolved

BrightQuest Treatment Centers. (2020, July 25). What is Attachment Trauma? –. https://www.brightquest.com/relational-trauma/what-is-attachment-trauma/

Childhelp National Child Abuse Hotline |. (n.d.). Https://Childhelphotline.Org/. Retrieved July 15, 2022, from https://childhelphotline.org/

ChoosingTherapy.com. (2022, May 10). Healing From Childhood Trauma: The Process & Effective Therapy Options. Choosing Therapy. https://www.choosingtherapy.com/healing-from-childhood-trauma/

Correlation Between Structures of the Brain Function and PTSD. (2020, February 13). Verywell Mind. https://www.verywellmind.com/what-exactly-does-ptsd-do-to-the-brain-2797210

Definition of mindfulness. (n.d.). Www.Dictionary.Com. Retrieved June 27, 2022, from https://www.dictionary.com/browse/mindfulness

Definition of trauma. (n.d.). Www.Dictionary.Com. Retrieved June 27, 2022, from https://www.dictionary.com/browse/trauma

Diagnostic and Statistical Manual of Mental Disorders - The DSM-5. (2019, April 30). The DSM5. https://www.thedsm5.com/the-dsm-5/

Domestic Violence Support | The National Domestic Violence Hotline. (2022, June 13). The Hotline. https://www.thehotline.org/

Four in 10 infants lack strong parental attachments. (2014, March 27). Princeton University. https://www.princeton.edu/news/2014/03/27/four-10-infants-lack-strong-parental-attachments

Gemma Stone. (2022, July). Overcoming Self-Sabotage. ToLoveThisLife.com. https://gemmastone.org/wp-content/uploads/2021/03/Overcome-Self-Sabotage-Workbook.pdf

Giourou, E., Skokou, M., Andrew, S. P., Alexopoulou, K., Gourzis, P., & Jelastopulu, E. (2018). Complex posttraumatic stress disorder: The need to consolidate a distinct clinical syndrome or to reevaluate features of psychiatric disorders following interpersonal trauma? World Journal of Psychiatry, 8(1), 12–19. https://doi.org/10.5498/wjp.v8.i1.12

Gotter, A. (2020, June 17). Box Breathing. Healthline. https://www.healthline.com/health/box-breathing

H. (n.d.-a). Cheryl Crumpler, PhD. Healthline. Retrieved July 28, 2022, from https://www.healthline.com/reviewers/cheryl-crumpler-phd

Sources

H. (n.d.-b). Crystal Hoshaw. Healthline. Retrieved July 28, 2022, from https://www.healthline.com/authors/crystal-hoshaw

Hoshaw, C. (2022, June 22). 32 Mindfulness Activities to Find Calm at Any Age. Healthline. https://www.healthline.com/health/mind-body/mindfulness-activities

How a Diagnosis of Complex PTSD Differs From PTSD. (2022, January 18). Verywell Mind. https://www.verywellmind.com/what-is-complex-ptsd-2797491

Khan, N. (2022, June 24). What Is Complex PTSD? | BetterHelp. Better Help. https://www.betterhelp.com/advice/ptsd/what-is-complex-ptsd/

Leonard, J. (2022, February 3). What is complex PTSD: Symptoms, treatment, and resources to help you cope. Medical News Daily. https://www.medicalnewstoday.com/articles/322886

Murphy, A. (2022, March 30). How to Stop Intrusive Thoughts: 8 Effective Ways. Declutter The Mind. https://declutterthemind.com/blog/how-to-stop-intrusive-thoughts/

Nanay Ph.D., B. (2022, June 22). How and Why EMDR Works. Psychology Today. https://www.psychologytoday.com/us/blog/psychology-tomorrow/202206/how-and-why-emdr-works

Özcan, N. K., Boyacioğlu, N. E., Enginkaya, S., Bilgin, H., & Tomruk, N. B. (2016). The relationship between attachment styles and childhood trauma: a transgenerational perspective - a controlled study of patients with psychiatric disorders. Journal of Clinical Nursing, 25(15–16), 2357–2366. https://doi.org/10.1111/jocn.13274

Post-traumatic stress disorder (PTSD) - Symptoms and causes. (2018, July 6). Mayo Clinic. https://www.mayoclinic.org/diseases-conditions/post-traumatic-stress-disorder/symptoms-causes/syc-20355967

Prevention, C. D. C. (n.d.). Fast Facts: Preventing Adverse Childhood Experiences |Violence Prevention|Injury Center|CDC. Centers for Disease Control and Prevention (CDC). Retrieved June 26, 2022, from https://www.cdc.gov/violenceprevention/aces/fastfact.html?CD C_AA_refVal=https%3A%2F%2Fwww.cdc.gov%2Fviolenceprev ention%2Facestudy%2Ffastfact.html

Psychology Today, P. (n.d.). Andrea Brandt Ph.D. M.F.T. Psychology Today. Retrieved July 29, 2022, from https://www.psychologytoday.com/us/contributors/andrea-brandt-phd-mft

Ryder, G. (2022, January 19). What Is Attachment Trauma? Psych Central. https://psychcentral.com/health/attachment-trauma

Suicide Prevention Lifeline. (n.d.). Suicide Prevention Lifeline. Retrieved June 27, 2022, from https://suicidepreventionlifeline.org/

Watson, S. (2021, July 20). Oxytocin: The love hormone. Harvard Health. https://www.health.harvard.edu/mind-and-mood/oxytocin-the-love-hormone

What Is Trauma Bonding? (2021, November 6). Verywell Mind. https://www.verywellmind.com/trauma-bonding-5207136

Wright LMFT, A. (2022, February 3). The Multifaceted Causes of C-PTSD, and Ways to Heal. Psychology Today. https://www.psychologytoday.com/us/blog/making-the-whole-beautiful/202202/the-multifaceted-causes-c-ptsd-and-ways-heal

Yoon, Susan, Ph.D. | College of Social Work- The Ohio State University. (n.d.). The Ohio State University. Retrieved July 27, 2022, from https://csw.osu.edu/about/faculty-staff/faculty-directory/yoon-susan-phd/

Resources

Books

- "The Body Keeps the Score" by Bessel van der Kolk, MD

- "It Didn't Start with You" by Mark Wolynn

- "Healing the Fragmented Selves of Trauma Survivors: Overcoming Internal Self-Alienation" by Janina Fisher, PhD

- "Trauma and Recovery" by Judith Lewis Herman, MD

- "The Complex PTSD Workbook" by Arielle Schwartz, PhD

- "Trauma and the Body" by Pat Ogden, PhD, Kekuni Minton, and Clare Pain

- "What Happened to You? Conversations on Trauma, Resilience, and Healing" by Bruce D. Perry, MD, PhD, and Oprah Winfrey

- "Waking the Tiger" by Peter Levine, PhD, with Ann Frederick

Helplines

- If you or a loved one are a victim of domestic violence or abuse, contact the National Domestic Violence Hotline at 1-800-799-7233 for confidential assistance from trained advocates.

- *Domestic Violence Support | The National Domestic Violence Hotline.* (2022, June 13). The Hotline. https://www.thehotline.org/

- For more mental health resources, see our National Helpline Database.

- *Childhelp National Child Abuse Hotline* |. (n.d.). Https://Childhelphotline.Org/. Retrieve July 15, 2022, from https://childhelphotline.org/

Made in United States
Troutdale, OR
11/13/2023

14546216R00119